Baedeker's
ISTANBUL

Imprint

Cover picture: View from the Beyazit Tower over the Covered Bazaar to the Blue Mosque (in the background Kadıköy on the Asiatic side of the Bosphorus)

120 colour photographs, 9 graphic representations, 10 special plans, 4 town plans

Text: Helmut Linde, Reutlingen

Consultants: Dr Bekir Yazgan and Leyla Özhan, Munich; Şerife Muslu, Istanbul
Editorial work: Baedeker Stuttgart
English language edition: Alec Court

Layout: Creativ GmbH, Ulrich Kolb, Stuttgart

General direction: Dr Peter Baumgarten, Baedeker Stuttgart

Cartography: Georg Schiffner, Lahr;
Huber & Oberländer, Munich;
Hallwag AG, Berne (city plan)

English translation: James Hogarth

Source of illustrations:
Baumgarten (1), Delta (2), Historia-Photo (9), Institut für Auslandsbeziehungen (3), Kalbfell (2), Keskin (16), Linde (52), Mayer (2), NET (4), Pfeffer (7), Richter (1), Schultheiss (15), Turkish Consulates General in Munich and Frankfurt am Main (7)

Following the tradition established by Karl Baedeker in 1844, sights of particular interest and hotels and restaurants of particular quality are distinguished by either one or two asterisks.

To make it easier to locate the various sights listed in the "A to Z" section of the Guide, their coordinates on the large city plan are shown in red at the head of each entry.

Only a selection of hotels and restaurants can be given: no reflection is implied, therefore, on establishments not included.

In a time of rapid change it is difficult to ensure that all the information given is entirely accurate and up to date, and the possibility of error can never be entirely eliminated. Although the publishers can accept no responsibility for inaccuracies and omissions, they are always grateful for corrections and suggestions for improvement.

© Baedeker Stuttgart
Original German edition

© 1987 Jarrold and Sons Ltd
English language edition world-wide

© 1987 The Automobile Association 57244
United Kingdom and Ireland

US and Canadian Edition
Prentice Hall Press

Licensed user:
Mairs Geographischer Verlag & Co., Ostfildern-Kemnat bei Stuttgart

Reproductions:
Gölz Repro-Service GmbH, Ostfildern-Kemnat bei Stuttgart

The name *Baedeker* is a registered trademark

Printed in Great Britain by Jarrold Printing, Norwich

0-13-058207-7 US & Canada

0 86145 412 X UK

3-87504-113-5 Germany

Contents

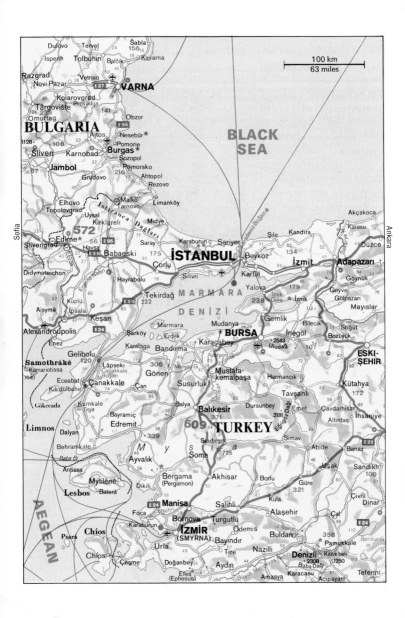

Preface

This Pocket Guide to Istanbul is one of the new generation of Baedeker guides.

Baedeker pocket guides, illustrated throughout in colour, are designed to meet the needs of the modern traveller. They are quick and easy to consult, with the principal features of interest described in alphabetical order and practical details about location, opening times, etc., shown in the margin.

Each city guide is divided into three parts. The first part gives a general account of the city, its history, notable personalities and so on; in the second part the principal sights are described; and the third part contains a variety of practical information designed to help visitors to find their way about and make the most of their stay.

The Baedeker pocket guides are noted for their concentration on essentials and their convenience of use. They contain numerous specially drawn plans and coloured illustrations, and at the back of the book is a large plan of the city. Each entry in the main part of the guide gives the coordinates of the square on the plan in which the particular feature can be located. Users of this guide, therefore, will have no difficulty in finding what they want to see.

Facts and Figures

General

Istanbul (Turkish İstanbul), known in antiquity as Byzantion
(Byzantium), later as Nova Roma or Constantinopolis (Constantinople), and finally as Istanbul (Stamboul), situated at the
point of junction between Europe and Asia, was the great
power centre of the Roman, Byzantine and Ottoman Empires.
Thanks to its situation at the intersection of the sea route from
the Mediterranean to the Black Sea and the land route from
south-eastern Europe into western Asia, and to its possession
of an excellent natural harbour (the Golden Horn), Istanbul
developed at an early stage into a commercial metropolis of the
first rank, which in spite of the loss of its function as a national
capital and its relegation to the status of a provincial capital has
lost little of its earlier importance. Indeed, Istanbul is still the
economic, cultural and spiritual capital of modern Turkey
(the seat of the Ecumenical Patriarch, high dignitaries of the
Eastern Churches, etc.).

Geographical situation

This fascinating city on the Bosphorus and the Golden Horn
lies between latitude 40°28' and 41°33' N and between
longitude 28°01' and 29°55' E. The highest point within the
immediate area of the city is Büyük Çamlıca (263 m (863 ft)),
with the Television Tower as a prominent landmark on its
summit.
Istanbul owes its incomparable character to the tripartite
division of the city area, laid out on hills (sometimes quite
steeply scarped) of schists and sedimentary rocks, by the Sea
of Marmara, the Bosphorus and the Golden Horn.
The city's original core lies on the peninsula washed by the Sea
of Marmara, the Bosphorus and the Golden Horn with its
characteristic seven hills, their rounded summits topped by
monumental buildings (the old Palace of the Sultans,
mosques). Tectonic processes (frequently earthquakes) and
variations in sea-level have brought about continual changes in
the coastline (leading, for example, to the silting up of the
ancient harbours). The western boundary of the old town is
formed by the old Byzantine land walls, now broken through at
a number of points to give passage to main roads.
Beyond the Golden Horn, now spanned by three bridges, rises
the port district of Galata established by the Genoese,
dominated by the massive Galata Tower. Higher up are suburbs
of almost Western European character – Beyoğlu, Osmanbey,
Şişli – with busy shopping streets, old embassy buildings,
churches, schools, theatres, banks, offices and modern hotels.
The outlying districts of Üsküdar, Haydarpaşa and Kadıköy on
the Asiatic side of the Bosphorus, once separate settlements,
have grown together into a single built-up area, with
extensions reaching out like fingers in all directions. The

◄ *Minaret of the Süleyman Mosque*

opening of the Bosphorus Bridge in 1973 gave a powerful impulse to the development of the Asiatic suburbs of Istanbul. Haydarpaşa is the terminus of the Anatolian and Baghdad Railway.

Climate

As a result of the nearness of the Black Sea and the Aegean the climate of Istanbul is marked by sharp contrasts. Although the average January temperature is 5·2 °C (41·4 °F) the winters can be severe, with much snow. The average temperature in August is 23·6 °C (74·5 °F). The summers are often muggy. The average annual rainfall is 635 mm (25 in), with the highest monthly figure in December.

Region

Province of Istanbul.

Telephone dialling codes

From the United Kingdom: 010 90 1
From the United States or Canada: 011 90 1
To the United Kingdom: 99 44
To the United States or Canada: 99 1

Administration

Istanbul lies within the province of the same name, which is divided into 16 districts. The head of the administration is the Vali (Governor).

Conurbation

The conurbation of Istanbul now extends in a swathe 40 km (25 miles) long and up to 10 km (6½ miles) wide from the European and northern Asiatic shores of the Sea of Marmara to about half-way along the Bosphorus (on both sides), its boundaries marked by the suburbs of Florya (European coast of Sea of Marmara), Bostancı (Asiatic coast of Sea of Marmara), Sarıryer (European side of Bosphorus) and Anadolukavak (Asiatic side of Bosphorus). The conurbation had an estimated population in 1983 of over 4·5 million, or roughly 10 per cent of the whole population of the Republic of Turkey. It is believed that during the warmer months of the year anything up to 6 million people are living on the Golden Horn, drawn by the manifold attractions of a cosmopolitan city.

Population and Religion

Population

The rise of the Greek city of Byzantion to become capital of the Eastern Roman Empire was accompanied by a steady increase in population. By about A.D. 400 it had probably reached the 200,000 mark. After passing through periods of decline the population rose again under Ottoman rule. At the beginning of the present century the number of inhabitants was well over a million. After the First World War and the transfer of the capital to Ankara there was a sharp decline in population, which in the 1920s fell below the 650,000 mark. The city's continuing role as the economic and cultural centre of Turkey, however, brought a recovery, and by 1935 the population had risen to 741,148. After the Second World War there was an influx of Turks from the Balkans, as well as a considerable inflow of population from the rural areas of Anatolia – a movement which is still continuing, bringing an annual population increase of between 80,000 and 100,000. The last population census in 1980 gave the population of Istanbul as 2,772,708. There are substantial ethnic minorities of Greeks, Armenians and Jews.

As a result of the rapid growth in population extensive areas of poor-quality housing (geçekondular) have grown up, particularly during the last 20 years or so, on the outskirts of the city, housing a population which is now well over 500,000. The municipal authorities are faced with great difficulties in preventing the further growth of these problem areas.

Geçekondular

Some 90 per cent of the city's population are Muslim. There are considerable minorities of Greek Orthodox, Armenian Christians, Catholics, Protestants and Jews.

Religion

Transport

Istanbul's international airport at Yeşilköy lies 15 km (9½ miles) west-south-west of the city centre, near the Sea of Marmara. It is Turkey's busiest airport, handling 2·5 million passengers in 1983. The Istanbul–Ankara, Istanbul–Bursa and Istanbul–İzmir connections are the busiest domestic routes.

Airport

Istanbul's port, as befits this old-established commercial and economic centre, is the largest and most important in Turkey, handling a large proportion of all the country's sea-borne exports and imports.
There are regular services from Istanbul to İzmir and Mersin on the Turkish Mediterranean coast, Famagusta (Turkish Gazi Mağusa) in northern Cyprus, Latakia in Syria and Trabzon on the Turkish Black Sea coast. The passenger harbour of Karaköy, at the north end of the Galata Bridge, has developed in recent

Port

A local steamer

Sirkeci Station

years into a busy port of call for cruise liners. Istanbul also features in the programme of many "fly and cruise" holidays (taking in, for example, the Danube, the Black Sea and Istanbul or the Eastern Mediterranean and Istanbul).

Rail services

Sirkeci Station, on the European side of the Bosphorus, has been since 1888 the terminus of European rail services. There are several trains daily between Central and Western European cities and Istanbul. In recent years the legendary Orient Express has been brought back into operation for the benefit of tourists, travelling down the historic route from various starting-points and at irregular intervals.

Haydarpaşa Station, on the Asiatic side, is the starting-point of the Anatolian railway network and the terminus of the Baghdad Railway, built at the beginning of this century by German engineers; it runs via Ankara to the Persian Gulf, continuing into Iraq.

European Highway 5 (E 5)

Since the completion of the new urban motorway, 22 km (14 miles) long, which runs round the north side of the city and spans both the Golden Horn and the Bosphorus on boldly engineered viaducts, European Highway 5 (E 5) is open to traffic all the way from the north of Europe to the Turkish-Syrian frontier.

National highways

1 (E 5N): Edirne–Lüleburgaz–Istanbul–Ankara
18 (E 5S): Alexandroupolis (GR)–Kesan (TR)–Tekirdağ–Istanbul
20: Istanbul–Kırklarelı–Edirne
25: Istanbul–Şile–Adapazarı

12

Roads along the Bosphorus:
Istanbul–Kilyos (European side)
Istanbul–Üsküdar–Beykoz (Asiatic side)

Transport within the city is provided by the buses of IETT, the municipal transport service. On some routes there are trolleybuses.

A major contribution is made to local transport by public taxis (dolmuş), which ply on fixed routes from and to squares in the city centre, taking on any passengers who hail them. They are an integral part of the Istanbul street scene, as are the countless ordinary taxis with their black and yellow markings.

The Tünel (Tunnel), Europe's oldest underground railway, runs between Karaköy and the end (63 m (207 ft) higher) of İstiklâl Caddesi, one of the city's principal shopping streets.

Turkish Railways operate suburban services between Sirkeci Station and Florya (European side) and between Haydarpaşa Station and Bostancı and Gebze (Asiatic side).

Much of the passenger traffic between the European and Asiatic parts of the city is carried by local steamers, plying between Kadıköy and Eminönü (or Sirkeci), at either end of the Galata Bridge.

Minibuses run between bus stations on the edge of the central area and the farther-out suburbs on both sides of the Bosphorus.

There are regular bus services between Istanbul and a number of major Central European cities, and also cities in western and southern Asia. The point of arrival and departure is the bus station outside the land walls at the Topkapı (Cannon Gate) on the west side of the city, the Topkapı Şehirlerarası Otobüs Terminalı.

Culture

For anyone concerned with the history of human culture, Istanbul is one of the world's most interesting cities, with monuments and works of art from different periods of history (antiquity, the Byzantine period and Ottoman times), more than 20 museums and numerous cultural institutions.

As in any cosmopolitan city, language need not be a problem for a visitor to Istanbul. He will find many people among the better-educated classes of the population with some knowledge of English or French, and large numbers of ordinary Turks have worked in Central European cities, particularly in West Germany, and have brought back a smattering of German.

Turkish itself belongs to the Turco-Tatar group of languages. Largely as a result of pressure by Atatürk, the modern language has discarded much of the Persian and Arabic vocabulary inherited from the past, and in recent years it has taken in many words from English and French.

Atatürk's introduction of the Latin alphabet in place of the old Arabic script has had very beneficial results, and has also made the language less daunting for foreigners.

Istanbul University was founded in 1863, and since then the city has acquired the University of Technology, the Marmara University and the Sinan University, as well as medical and veterinary schools, colleges of technology, international commerce and art, various other technical colleges and foreign schools of archaeology and cultural institutes.

Theatres and concerts

Some 30 municipal and privately run theatres, including the Opera House (Atatürk Kültür Sarayı) in Taksim Square, which was reopened in 1976, provide a varied range of theatrical entertainment; and the Municipal Symphony Orchestra has established a reputation which extends well beyond the boundaries of Turkey.

Istanbul Festival

The Istanbul Festival, established in 1973, runs from mid June to mid July, offering a full programme of musical and dramatic events, with theatrical companies, orchestras and soloists from many different countries, as well as performances of Turkish folk-dances and shadow plays.

Commerce and Industry

Istanbul is Turkey's leading industrial and commercial centre, with some 40 per cent of all Turkish industrial firms based in the city, in a range which extends from the production of high-quality textiles to heavy industry (iron and steel, shipbuilding). Craft production is also very active, not only meeting the everyday needs of the city's population but also supplying industry. For many centuries, too, Istanbul has been famed as a commercial metropolis, a status symbolised by its possession of the world's largest bazaar. Most Turkish wholesalers have their headquarters or their principal branches in the city. In recent years there has been a very considerable growth in the tertiary sector of the economy (services), largely due to the enormous expansion in the volume of exports. This is also reflected in Istanbul's position as a banking centre. Interpreters, brokers, lawyers and insurance agents are now essential elements in the increasingly complex economic structures of the city.

Industrial structure

As already noted, practically the whole range of Turkish industry – which is very young, having begun to develop only in the 1950s – is represented in Istanbul. Traditional branches of industry are iron and steel, shipbuilding, building and foodstuffs.

In recent years consumer goods manufacture, much of it exported, has been concentrated in the Istanbul area, favoured by Turkey's treaty of association with the European Economic Community and by special trade agreements with the Federal Republic of Germany. Some 75 per cent of all employment in the production of high-class textiles, furs and leather goods, the chemical industry, electronics and the graphic trades is in the Istanbul conurbation, and some 50 per cent of Turks employed in the automobile and engineering industries work in Istanbul. Other rapidly developing branches of industry are glass, ceramics, optical products and precision engineering. Given the relatively low level of wages in Turkey and its almost inexhaustible resources of manpower, firms in Western and Central Europe are increasingly having high-quality products (fine fashion textiles, furs, leather jackets, shoes, costume jewellery, crystal, etc.) manufactured in the Istanbul area.

From time immemorial most of the city's craft production and industry has been concentrated round the world's largest bazaar and along the shores of the Golden Horn, but a newer industrial zone has developed between the higher part of the city with its administrative and commercial functions (and also some of the residential areas favoured by the middle and upper ranks of the population) and the shanty town areas with their reservoir of cheap labour. The most recent tendency is to create industrial "axes of development" along the main trunk roads, a striking example being the development that has taken place along the E 5 from Üsküdar to Ankara, where factories and industrial establishments at all stages of development extend for a distance of some 40 km (25 miles). The same thing can be seen along the roads to the west of Istanbul.

Industrial areas

The rapid pace of industrialisation in the last three decades has had gravely deleterious effects on the environment. Worst hit has been the Golden Horn, the waters of which are now, for all practical purposes, dead.

Environmental problems

Notable Personalities

Mustafa Kemal Paşa, better known as Atatürk, was born in Salonica and died in Istanbul. In his youth he was a leading member of the Young Turks, fought against the Italians in the Tripoli War (1911) and commanded a Turkish force in the Dardanelles during the First World War. When western Turkey was occupied by the Greeks in 1918 he withdrew to Asia Minor. In 1922 he defeated the Greeks, and a year later proclaimed the Turkish Republic, of which he became first President. He made Ankara the new Turkish capital and carried through a series of political and social reforms (administration of justice, position of women, alphabet, language, calendar, dress).

*Atatürk
(1880–1938)*

Byzas, the legendary founder of Byzantion, is said to have been the leader of a group of Megarians who, following a direction from the Oracle of Delphi, founded a settlement in the 7th c. B.C. on the wedge-shaped strip of land between the Golden Horn and the Sea of Marmara, opposite the earlier Greek colony of Chalcedon (now Kadıköy) on the Asiatic side of the Bosphorus.

*Byzas
(c. 658 B.C)*

The Emperor Constantine I, the Great, born in what is now Niš in Serbia, transferred the capital of the Empire in 330 from Rome to Byzantium, which was now called Nova Roma (New Rome) or Constantinopolis. With the promulgation of the Edict of Milan (313), granting tolerance to the Christian religion, he took the first step towards making Christianity the State religion of the Empire.
During his reign the foundation-stone of Haghia Sophia was laid, the Forum was completed and the Hippodrome was embellished with the Serpent Column from Delphi. Constantine is a saint of the Armenian and Greek and Russian Orthodox Churches.

*Constantine I
(c. 288–337)*

The Persian King Darius I, one of the greatest rulers of the ancient East, was a member of the Achaemenid dynasty. He

*Darius
(550–486 B.C.)*

15

Notable Personalities

Atatürk

Mehmet the Conqueror

Süleyman the Magnificent

extended the Persian Empire to the Indus, and in 513 B.C., during a campaign against the Scythians, crossed the Bosphorus on a bridge of boats, the legendary forerunner of the present Bosphorus Bridge, the fourth-longest suspension bridge in the world.

Eyüp
(c. A.D. 674)

Eyüp Ensarî, a close friend of the Prophet Muhammad and standard-bearer of Islam's earliest military forces, was an army commander during the First Arab Siege of Constantinople in 674–678. He is said to have been killed during the fighting and to have been buried on the site of the present Eyüp Mosque, which ranks fourth among the holy places of Islam, after Mecca, Medina and Jerusalem.

Colmar, Freiherr von der Goltz
(1843–1916)

This Prussian Field-Marshal was responsible for rebuilding the Turkish army between 1883 and 1895 and was granted the title of Pasha. He commanded a Turkish force in Mesopotamia in 1915–16, and died in Baghdad in 1916.

Osman Hamdi Bey
(1842–1910)

Osman Hamdi Bey, born in Istanbul, did much to foster the cultural life of the capital. In 1880 he established a college of art, and in the following year promoted the foundation of a museum of art in Istanbul. He played a major part in the archaeological investigation of Sidon, where the Alexander Sarcophagus now in the Archaeological Museum was discovered.

Justinian I
(483–565)

Justinian, Eastern Roman Emperor from 527 to 565, succeeded in bringing under his rule many of the Germanic tribes who were harrying the Western Empire and carried through the great codification of Roman law associated with his name. Among the major building projects undertaken in Constantinople during his reign were the enlargement of Haghia Sophia, the Church of Haghia Eirene, the Monastery of St Saviour in Chora, the Church of SS. Sergius and Bacchus and the Forum Augusteum.

Namık Kemal
(1840–88)

The writer Namık Kemal, born in Tekirdağ, was one of the fiercest opponents of the despotism of the Ottoman Sultans. One of his plays gave rise to an uproar in the Gedikpaşa Theatre, and in 1873 he was exiled to Cyprus. He was one of the founders of the Young Turks, established in Paris about 1876.

16

The Istanbul poet Necip Fazıl Kisakurek was one of the pioneers of modern Turkish lyric poetry. At first he reacted strongly against the Ottoman poetry of his day, but later returned to Ottoman traditions, achieving a considerable reputation among traditionally minded Turks.

Necip Fazıl Kisakurek
(1905–83)

Pierre Loti, born at Rochefort in western France, became a naval officer and made his name as a writer. Pierre Loti was a pseudonym: his real name was Julien Viaud. He visited Constantinople in the time of the Ottoman Sultans, and a number of his romantic novels have the city as their setting ("Aziyadé", "Fantôme d'Orient").

Pierre Loti
(1850–1923)

The Turkish Sultan Mehmet II Fâtih (the Conqueror), born in Edirne (Adrianople), took Constantinople in 1453, after which the city became known as Stamboul (Istanbul). He was the seventh Sultan of the Ottoman Empire, reigning from 1451 to 1481. During his reign the first Ottoman palace on the European shores of the Bopsphorus was built.

Mehmet II Fâtih
(1430–81)

Born at Kayseri in Anatolia, Sinan Ağa became the most celebrated Turkish architect. He entered the service of the Ottoman rulers as a janissary and military engineer, and in 1534 became Architect to the Sultan. More than 330 buildings are attributed to him or to his school, including more than 80 mosques, over 50 schools and more than 30 palaces. Among his principal works are the Süleyman Mosque in Istanbul and the Selim Mosque in Edirne.

Sinan Ağa
(1499–1588)

Sultan Süleyman Kanuni, the Magnificent, was the most active of the Ottoman rulers. In 1526 he conquered Hungary, and in 1529 reached the very gates of Vienna. His Empire extended far into Persia, and his fleets controlled practically the whole of the Mediterranean and the Red Sea. During his reign Istanbul flourished as never before, a prosperity reflected in furious building activity (in which Sinan played a great part).

Süleyman the Magnificent
(1494–1566)

Theodosius the Great, a native of Cauca in Spain, succeeded Valens as Eastern Roman Emperor in 379. In 381 he held the Second Ecumenical Council in Constantinople and proclaimed Christianity the State religion. In 382 he concluded a treaty with the Goths, and in 394 united the Roman Empire under a single ruler for the last time. He enriched his capital by the construction of the Golden Gate and the erection of an obelisk from Luxor.

Theodosius I
(347–395)

Theodora, daughter of a circus attendant and herself a notorious dancer, became the wife of the Emperor Justinian I in 527. A woman of considerable gifts, she had much influence on his decisions, and encouraged him to resist the Nika Insurrection. She is credited with the establishment of the world's first secret service.

Theodora
(c. 497–548)

The Istanbul lyric poet Mehmet Emin Yurdakul was an ardent supporter of Turkish nationalism. His poems, written in simple language, are still popular.

Mehmet Emin Yurdakul
(1869–1944)

History of Istanbul

Neolithic period	First traces of human occupation.
Transition from Bronze Age to Iron Age	Evidence of human activity on the site now occupied by the Archaeological Museum.
c. 660 B.C.	Dorian Greeks found Byzantion.
512 B.C.	King Darius I of Persia throws a bridge of boats over the Bosphorus and takes Byzantion.
479 B.C.	The Spartan leader Pausanias frees the city from the Persian yoke.
339 B.C.	Philip II of Macedon besieges Byzantion, without success.
278 B.C.	The town is plundered by the Galatians, a Celtic tribe, who settle in Thrace.
146 B.C.	The free city of Byzantion concludes a treaty with Rome.
A.D. 192–196	Septimius Severus besieges Byzantium, which had supported a rival Emperor.
269	Claudis II repels the Goths.
324	The Emperor Constantine takes the city and, recognising the advantages of its situation on the threshold of the East, makes it the second capital of the Roman Empire.
330	The city is renamed Nova Roma (New Rome), but soon becomes known as Constantinopolis. It is now the undisputed capital of the Roman Empire.
395	The sons of Theodosius I divide the Empire. Arcadius makes Constantinople capital of the Eastern Roman Empire.
408–450	In the reign of Theodosius II the city is strongly fortified (land walls on the west side, sea walls along the Sea of Marmara and the Golden Horn).
527–565	Constantinople flourishes during the reign of Justinian I. Haghia Sophia, the Church of the Holy Wisdom, is completed. A distinctive Byzantine culture develops.
532	Devastation following the Nika Insurrection.
7th–10th c.	The city is harried by Avars, Persians and Arabs.
674–678	Arab siege of Constantinople, in the course of which Eyüp Ensarî, a close friend of the Prophet Muhammad, is killed.
8th–9th c.	The Iconoclast conflict (between the opponents and the supporters of images and relics).
813	The Bulgars besiege Constantinople.
924	Second Bulgar Siege.

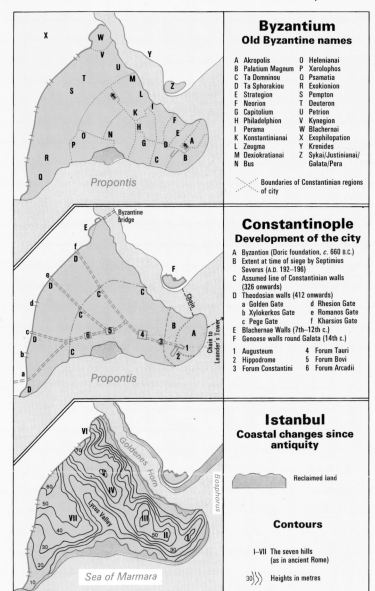

Byzantium
Old Byzantine names

A Akropolis
B Palatium Magnum
C Ta Domninou
D Ta Sphorakiou
E Strategion
F Neorion
G Capitolium
H Philadelphion
I Perama
K Konstantinianai
L Zeugma
M Dexiokratianai
N Bus
O Helenianai
P Xerolophos
Q Psamatia
R Exokionion
S Pempton
T Deuteron
U Petrion
V Kynegion
W Blachernai
X Exophilopation
Y Krenides
Z Sykai/Justinianai/ Galata/Pera

Boundaries of Constantinian regions of city

Constantinople
Development of the city

A Byzantion (Doric foundation, c. 660 B.C.)
B Extent at time of siege by Septimius Severus (A.D. 192–196)
C Assumed line of Constantinian walls (326 onwards)
D Theodosian walls (412 onwards)
  a Golden Gate   d Rhesion Gate
  b Xylokerkos Gate e Romanos Gate
  c Pege Gate   f Kharsios Gate
E Blachernae Walls (7th–12th c.)
F Genoese walls round Galata (14th c.)

1 Augusteum
2 Hippodrome
3 Forum Constantini
4 Forum Tauri
5 Forum Bovi
6 Forum Arcadii

Istanbul
Coastal changes since antiquity

Reclaimed land

Contours

I–VII The seven hills (as in ancient Rome)

30 Heights in metres

19

History of Istanbul

11th–12th c.	Growth of Genoese, Pisan and Venetian influence.
1048	Russian fleet off Constantinople.
11th c.	The Eastern Empire is threatened by the Seljuks in the east and the Italian maritime cities in the west.
1054	The Patriarch of Constantinople, Michael Caerulareus, and Pope Leo IX excommunicate one another. The long-threatened schism between the Greek Orthodox and Roman Catholic Churches finally comes about.
1204	Crusaders plunder Constantinople and instal a Latin Emperor.
1261	The Greek Emperor Michael VIII Palaeologus expels the Latins with the help of the Genoese, who in return are granted possession of Galata.
13th–15th c.	The Turks advance on Constantinople.
1361	In the reign of Murat I the Sultan's residence is moved from Bursa to Edirne (Adrianople).
1422	Constantinople is encircled by the Turks.
1453	Mehmet II (Fâtih, the Conqueror) takes Constantinople, now to be named Istanbul.
1454	Istanbul supersedes Edirne as capital of the Ottoman Empire.
15th–16th c.	Istanbul flourishes. Vigorous building activity, particularly during the reigns of Sultans Selim I and Süleyman the Magnificent. The great architect Sinan leaves his mark on the city with his mosques.
18th c.	Economic recession. In spite of this a number of notable buildings, showing Baroque influence, are erected.
18th–19th c.	After the Turkish withdrawal from Eastern Central Europe and the fall of the Ottoman Empire the phrase "the stick man of Europe" comes into use.
1780–1807	Sultan Selim III attempts to introduce reforms on the Western European, and particularly the French, pattern but is frustrated by the resistance of the conservative Janissaries.
1826–27	Sultan Mahmut destroys the Janissaries.
1853–56	Crimean War.
1875	The economic situation of the Ottoman Empire deteriorates still further. The European colonial powers increase their influence.
1877	Opening of the first Turkish Parliament.
1877–78	Russo-Turkish War.
1888	Istanbul is linked with the European railway network.
1898	The German Emperor, William II, visits Constantinople, emphasising the importance of German-Turkish co-operation.

Construction of the railway line from Istanbul's Asiatic suburb of Haydarpaşa to Baghdad, with German assistance.	1902
The Young Turks oppose the Sultan's absolutist rule and campaign for a Turkish national state.	1900–09
Coup d'état of the Young Turks.	1913
Istanbul is temporarily occupied by Allied forces. It is planned to make it part of a Greater Greece.	First World War (1914–18)
Mustafa Kemal Paşa (Atatürk) proclaims the Turkish Republic and moves the capital to Ankara.	1923
Atatürk dies in the Dolmabahçe Palace.	1938
During the 1940s large-scale slum clearance operations are carried out and new traffic arteries such as Atatürk Bulvarı and Eminönü Meydanı are opened up.	Second World War (1939–45)
Construction of the Atatürk Palace of Culture.	1946–60
Second slum clearance programme. Irreplaceable old buildings are pulled down to make way for more new traffic arteries.	1956–59
After the difficulties of integrating some 300,000 Turkish refugees from the Balkans after the Second World War Istanbul is faced with almost insoluable problems by the great influx of population from rural areas.	1960 onwards
The Bosphorus Bridge, one of the world's longest suspension bridges, is opened to traffic.	1973
A ship is wrecked to the south of Leander's Tower, with the loss of 51 lives; oil pollution at the south end of the Bosphorous.	1979
Important exhibitions in Istanbul, "Anatolian Civilisations" and "Islamic Art".	1983
New terminal at Yeşilköy Airport comes into operation.	1984

Byzantine Emperors

306–337	Constantine I
337–361	Constantine II
361–363	Julian the Apostate
363–364	Jovian
364–378	Valens
378–395	Theodosius the Great
395–408	Arcadius
408–450	Theodosius II
450–457	Marcian
457–474	Leo I
474–491	Zeno
491–518	Anastasius I
518–527	Justin I
527–565	Justinian I
565–578	Justin II

Byzantine Emperors

Constantine

Theodosius

Justinian

Byzantine Emperors
(continued)

578–582	Tiberius I Constantine
582–602	Maurice
602–610	Phocas
610–641	Heraclius
641	Constantine II
641	Heracleonas
641–668	Constantine III
668–695	Constantine IV
685–695	Justinian II
695–698	Leontius
698–705	Tiberius II Apsimar
705–711	Justinian II (second reign)
711–713	Philippicus Bardanes
713–715	Anastasius II
715–717	Theodosius III
717–741	Leo III
741–775	Constantine V
775–780	Leo IV
780–797	Constantine VI
797–802	Irene
802–811	Nicephorus I
811–813	Michael I
813–820	Leo V
820–829	Michael II
829–842	Theophilus
842–867	Michael III
867–886	Basil I
886–912	Leo VI
912–913	Alexander
913–959	Constantine VII Porphyrogenitus (Romanus I Lecapenus co-Emperor 919–944)
959–963	Romanus II Phocas
963–969	Nicephorus II Phocas
969–976	John I Tzimisces
976–1025	Basil II
1025–28	Constantine VIII
1028–34	Romanus III Argyrus
1034–41	Michael IV
1041–42	Michael V
1042	Theodora and Zoe

1042–55	Constantine IX
1055–56	Theodora (second reign)
1056–57	Michael VI
1057–59	Isaac I Comnenus
1059–67	Constantine X Ducas
1067	Eudocia Ducaena
1068–71	Romanus IV Diogenes
1071–78	Michael VII Ducas
1078–81	Nicephorus III Botaniates
1081–1118	Alexius I Comnenus
1118–43	John II Comnenus
1143–80	Manuel I Comnenus
1180–83	Alexius II Comnenus
1183–85	Andronicus I Comnenus
1185–95	Isaac II Angelus
1195–1203	Alexius III Angelus
1203–04	Isaac II Angelus (second reign; Alexius IV Angelus co-Emperor)
1204	Alexius V Ducas
1204–22	Theodore I Lascaris (in Nicaea)
1222–54	John III Ducas Vatatzes (in Nicaea)
1254–58	Theodore II Lascaris (in Nicaea)
1258–61	John IV Lascaris (in Nicaea)
1261–82	Michael VIII Palaeologus
1282–1328	Andronicus II Palaeologus
1328–41	Andronicus III Palaeologus
1341–91	John V Palaeologus
1347–54	John VI Cantacuzene (Anti-Emperor)
1376–79	Andronicus IV Palaeologus
1390	John VII Palaeologus
1391–1425	Manuel II Palaeologus
1425–48	John VII Palaeologus
1448–53	Constantine XI Dragases

Latin Emperors

1204–05	Baldwin of Flanders
1206–16	Henry of Flanders
1217	Peter of Courtenay
1217–19	Yolande
1221–28	Robert of Courtenay
1228–61	Baldwin II (1231–37 John of Brienne)

Ottoman Sultans

1453–81	Mehmet II (Fâtih, the Conqueror)
1481–1512	Beyazit II
1512–20	Selim I
1520–66	Süleyman I (Kanuni, the Magnificent)
1566–74	Selim II
1574–95	Murat III
1595–1603	Mehmet III
1603–17	Ahmet I
1617–18	Mustafa I
1618–22	Osman II
1622–23	Mustafa I (second reign)

Ottoman Sultans

1623–40	Murat IV
1640–48	İbrahim (the Terrible)
1648–87	Mehmet IV
1687–91	Süleyman II
1691–95	Ahmet II
1695–1703	Mustafa II
1703–30	Ahmet III
1730–54	Mahmut I
1754–57	Osman III
1757–74	Mustafa III
1774–89	Abdül Hamit I
1789–1807	Selim III
1807–08	Mustafa IV
1808–39	Mahmut II
1839–61	Abdül Mecit I
1861–76	Abdül Aziz
1876	Murat V
1876–1909	Abdül Hamit II
1909–18	Mehmet V
1918–22	Mehmet VI
1922–23	Abdül Mecit II (Caliph only)

Quotations

"In situation and architecture Istanbul is surely the most fairy-tale-like place in the world.

There is a Turkish tale that Napoleon III once assembled the ambassadors of many different countries and asked them which was the best or strongest State in the world. He expected compliments for France, and these were readily provided on all sides. The only exception was Ali Pasha, who said, 'Turkey.' 'Why?' he was asked. 'Because,' he said, 'you outside the country, and we inside it, have been doing our best for the last hundred years to destroy it – and we have not succeeded.'

Much the same could be said about the townscape of Istanbul. For the last hundred years industry, speculators, public authorities and private citizens have been doing their utmost to destroy the city's beauty; but so far they have not succeeded. Thanks to its situation, even the appalling jumble of buildings in Pera looks beautiful when seen across the water in the morning sunshine. This God-given situation with its long waterfronts, its hills and its inlets crowded with boats has triumphed over the evil intentions of men – so far. But we ought not to try God's patience too far."

Paul Bonatz
German architect
(1877–1956)

"The walls of the Seraglio are like the walls of Newstead Gardens, only higher, and much in the same order, but the ride by the walls of the city on the land side is beautiful, imagine, four miles of immense triple battlements covered with ivy, surmounted with 218 towers, and on the other side of the road Turkish burying-grounds (the loveliest spots on earth) full of enormous cypresses. I have seen the ruins of Athens, of Ephesus, and Delphi, I have traversed great party of Turkey and many other parts of Europe and some of Asia, but I never beheld a work of Nature or Art which yielded an impression like the propspect on each side, from the Seven Towers to the end of the Golden Horn."

George Gordon, Lord Byron
English poet
(1788–1824)

"What has been said about the beauty of the Bosphorus is – including the exaggeration – literally true, for exaggeration is natural to elevation. At first, feeling out of sorts. I could not enjoy it, but soon the impression became so powerful that I gave mysef wholly up to it. The situation of Constantinople has been preferred to that of Naples, perhaps wrongly so far as concerns beauty; but it is more extensive, on a larger scale, and thereby more powerful. For almost four hours' travelling fortifications, castles, villages and palaces follow one another, first only on the European side and then on the Asiatic side as well, in unbroken and delightful succession. The world has perhaps nothing that, as a whole, can be compared with it. Looked at individually, only the castles have merit in themselves. The palaces of the Turks are no more than a huddling together of summer-houses. Their way of life shows even in luxury that their requirements are modest. And then all these buildings are of wood. I confess that when I was told this it took away half my pleasure. From a distance, however, and before you hear things like that it all looks magnificent. And so it continues, with the same unbroken succession of fortifications and batteries on either side. The charming village of Büyükdere, Therapia, the European and the Asiatic castle, Leander's Tower – now, I think a hospital. Beyond all this

Franz Grillparzer
Austrian writer
(1791–1872)

Quotations

Lord Byron

Franz Grillparzer

Helmuth von Moltke

the tip of the Seraglio with its walls, which resemble folding screens. And to the rear a glimpse of the dome of St Sophia. . . ."

Alexander von Humboldt
German scientist and
traveller
(1769–1869)

"Istanbul . . . the most beautiful city in the world!"

Lord Kinross
English writer
"Europa Minor"
(referring to visits in
1947–54)

"Istanbul is in effect two cities, divided by the Golden Horn. One is Pera, now Beyoğlu, the ill-planned jangling city of the Europeans; the other is Stamboul, the more spacious city of Byzantium, with its incomparable skyline of mosques. Pera is a nineteenth-century quarter, with narrow canyons of cobbled lanes careering headlong down to the water. Its ponderous tenements, gaping obscenely, ring with the clangour of trams and the grinding of gears, as the traffic hurries irritably upwards and downwards through precipitous winding streets. Until horns were forbidden it was a pandemonium of noise; now this is replaced by a tattoo, as the drivers, rather than run down the crowds, beat with their hands on the sides of their vehicles. The long narrow rue de Pera, the most ignoble of international streets, bustles all day long with office crowds, swarming into the milk bars and the sausage shops and the shoeshine parlours which now supplement, in the German-American manner, the more sedate Turkish cafés of the past. From the top of it a new city of modern apartment blocks and streamlined public buildings spreads out over the hillsides, beyond the spacious Taksim Gardens, its well-planned boulevards curving downwards to the Bosphorus below.

From the sombre warehouses and quays of Galata, with their murky cafés, the Galata Bridge floats low over the Golden Horn, through a forest of masts and sails and funnels from the shipping packed close in the harbour. By the bridgehead the Valide Mosque, with its pyramid of domes and its minarets, like lighthouses, commands the approach to the Muslim city with a calm and spacious dignity.

The skyline of Istanbul is still inherently that of Byzantium. Eliminate the pencilled minarets and it becomes a city of domes, looking much as it might have done had the Byzantine Empire survived for another few centuries."

"But how shall I describe to you the charm in which we were now enfolded? From the rawness of winter we had been transported into the mildest of summers, from a desert into the most vigorous life. The sun shone brightly and warmly in the sky, and only a thin mist cast a transparent veil over the fairy-like scene. To the right we had Constantinople with its colourful mass of houses, above which rose countless domes, the boldly engineered arches of an aqueduct, huge stone hans with lead roofs and above all the soaring minarets surrounding the seven gigantic mosques of Selim, Mehmet, Süleyman, Beyazit, Valide, Ahmet and Sophia. The old Seraglio extends far out into the sea with its fantastic kiosks and domes, its black cypresses and mighty plane trees. The waves of the Bosphorus beat against the promontory, breaking into foam under the old walls. Beyond this is the Propontis with its groups of islands and rocky coasts. The eye returns from these misty distances and fixes on the beautiful mosques of Scutari or Üsküdar, once known as Chrysopolis, now an Asiatic suburb of the city; on the Maiden's Tower, rising out of deep water between Europe and Asia; on the hills, still freshly green; and on the great cemetery areas in the shade of the cypresses."

Helmuth von Moltke
German officer
(1800–91)

'This Citie by destinie appointed, and by nature seated for Soveraigntie, was first the seat of the Romane Emperors, then of the Greeke, as now it is of the Turkish: built by Constantine the Sonne of Helena, and lost by Constantine the Sonne of another Helena . . . to Mahomet the second, in the yeare 1453, with the slaughter of her people and destruction of her magnificent structures. . . .
It stands on a Cape of Land neere the entrance of the Bosphorus. In forme triangular, on the East-side washed with the same, and on the North-side with the Haven, adjoyning on the West to the Continent. Walled bricke and stone, intermixed orderly, having four and twentie gates and posternes; whereof five doe regard the Land, and nineteene the water, being about thirteene miles in circumference. Than this there is hardly in nature a more delicate Object, if beheld from the Sea or adjoyning Mountaines; the loftie and beautifull Cypresse Trees so intermixed with the buildings, that it seemeth to present a Citie in a Wood to the pleased beholders. Whose seven aspiring heads (for on so many hils and no more, they say it is seated) are most of them crowned with magnificent Mosques, all of white Marble, round in forme, and coupled above; being finished on the top with gilded Spires, that reflect the beames they receive with a marvellous splendour; some having two, some foure, some sixe adjoyning Turrets, exceeding high and exceeding slender. . . ."

George Sandys
English poet and traveller
(1578–1644)
Account of a visit in 1610

Sights from A to Z

For technical and topographical terms see Practical Information – Language.

Note

---

* Ahmet III Çeşmesi (Fountain of Ahmet III)

E8

This fountain, set up by Sultan Ahmet III in 1728 – during the
heyday of Ottoman Rococo – is one of the finest of its kind in
Istanbul. It has recently been restored.
The elaborate fountain-house has little oriel windows with
bronze grilles at the corners and a curved overhanging roof
surmounted by five charming little domes, and is decorated
with calligraphic inscriptions, tiles and finely worked patterns
in relief. The four wall-fountains are set within niches.

Location
Çeşme Sok

Bus stop
Sultanahmet

Ahmet Pasa Camii (Ahmet Paşa Mosque; also known as Topkapi Camii)

C2

The Ahmet Paşa Mosque was built in the 16th c. by the
celebrated architect Sinan for Kara Ahmet Paşa, Grand Vizier to
Sultan Süleyman the Magnificent. In the course of its history it
has several times been altered. Built on a square plan, it has four
semi-domes at the corners which give it its distinctive aspect.
The main dome is borne on arches which are themselves
supported on six columns.
The ornament on the mimber and the decoration of the roof
over the muezzin's platform are particularly fine. The beautifully
patterned glazed tiles are characteristic of the great period of
Ottoman faience in the 16th c.
The medrese in the (relatively large) courtyard of the mosque
is particularly attractive following recent renovation work.

Location
Topkapı Cad.

Bus stop
Topkapı

Alay Köskü (Alay Pavilion)

D8

The Alay Pavilion was built for Sultan Mahmut II in 1810 at a
corner on the west wall of the Seraglio, opposite the Bab-ı ali
(see entry), so that he could watch parades from there.
(*Alay*=procession, regiment.) This richly decorated little
building, on a polygonal plan, has been occupied since 1970
by the Kenan Ozbel Collection (carpets and kilims; textiles;
sculpture; ceramics; needlework).

Location
SW corner of Gülhane Parkı

Bus stop
Gülhane Parkı

---

* Amcazade Hüseyin Pasa Medresesi
(Türk İnşaat Sanatları Müzesi: Building Museum)

D5

This medrese is part of the extensive Amcazade complex
founded in the 17th c. by Sultan Mustafa II's Grand Vizier, one
of the finest Baroque foundations of its kind in Istanbul.

Location
Macarkardeşler Cad.

◀ *Yeni Cami (New Mosque)*

Amcazade Hüseyin Pasa Medresesi

Fountain of Ahmet III

The medrese now houses a museum which offers an interesting survey, in 13 sections, of the development of Turkish building techniques. The exhibits include not only paving, masonry, arches, capitals, friezes, stone inscriptions, bricks, stuccowork, timber and iron structures but also wall tiles from the workshops of İznik and Kütahya. Also of great interest are the displays of building elements and accessories (nails, cramps, locks, measuring instruments; marble slabs, well foundations; lamps, candlesticks, rose-water basins, etc.).

Bus stop
Fâtih

Opening times
Tues.–Sun. 9 a.m.–5 p.m.

Anadolu Hisarı (Castle)

The Fortress of Anadolu Hisarı, on the Asiatic side of the Bosphorus, was built by Yıldırım Beyazit I at the end of the 14th c. and enlarged and strengthened in the time of Mehmet the Conqueror (mid 15th c.). Together with Rumeli Hisarı (see entry) on the European side it was designed to close the Bosphorus to passage by the Byzantines. After the Conquest of Constantinople by the Turks in 1453 it had no further purpose and was allowed to fall into a state of dilapidation, to be restored only in recent times.
The central feature of the fortress is a massive keep, round which are an inner circuit of walls, with four towers, and an outer circuit with three.

Location
Anadolu Hisarı

Bus stop
Anadolu Hisarı

Boat landing-stage
Anadolu Hisarı

Ancient Orient, Museum of the

See Arkeoloji Müzesi, Eski Şark Eserleri Müzesi

Aqueduct of Valens

See Bozdoğan Kemeri

Arap Camii (Arab Mosque)   C7

Legend has it that the Arap Camii was built during the Siege of Constantinople by the Arabs under the leadership of Maslama in 717–718 (see inscription on south wall). Against this, architectural evidence indicates that the mosque occupies the site of an earlier Christian church known under the Latin Emperors as SS. Paolo e Domenico. More than a hundred tombstones from the church can be seen in the Archaeological Museum (see Arkeoloji Müzesi). The church was converted into a mosque by Mehmet the Conqueror. Since then it has several times been restored.

Location
Abdüsselah Sok

Bus stop
Karaköy

*Arasta Mozaik Müzesi (Mosaic Museum)   E7/8

During excavations in 1935 near the Sultan Ahmet Mosque a number of fine mosaic pavements, originally in the peristyle of

Location
Sultanahmet

Bus stop
Sultanahmet

Opening times
Tues.–Sun. 9 a.m.–5 p.m.

a Byzantine imperial palace, were brought to light. The mosaics, which date from the 4th and 5th c., depict animals fighting, plants and mythological scenes. In the exhibition rooms adjoining the site are mosaics of various periods.

Arkeoloji Müzesi (Archaeological Museum)   **D8**

Location
Gülhane Parkı

Bus stops
Eminönü, Sultanahmet,
Gülhane Parkı

Opening times
Tues.–Sun. 9.30 a.m.–5 p.m.

Admission charge

Charge for photography

The Archaeological Museum of Istanbul is one of the great archaeological museums of the world. Its origins go back to a collection of antiquities established by Damat Fethi Paşa in 1846 and considerably enlarged by Maarif Naziri Saffet between 1869 and 1871. The museum, which acquired its own premises in 1896, gained international reputation under its Director Osman Hamdi Bey, who directed the excavations of Sidon and secured some items of superlative quality for the museum.

The museum is at present being enlarged at considerable expense. It occupies the site of various buildings of the Early Byzantine period, including a church, remains of which were found during excavation work for the new building.

Of the museum's many treasures only a selection of outstanding items can be mentioned here.

Room 1:
Funerary stelae of the 3rd and 4th c. B.C., those of Hecatodorus (No. 4206), Theodotus (No. 4845), Musa (No. 5024) and Lollia Salbia (No. 5547) being particularly fine; statues found at the Theodosian land walls, including figures of Artemis and Heracles.

Room 2:
Fragments of a frieze from the Temple of Artemis Leucophryne in Magnesia on the Maeander; fragments of a frieze from the Temple of Hecate, Lagina; various capitals and column bases, including a figure of Eros surrounded by wild beasts and marine monsters (No. 1642), a capital from Larissa (No. 1924) and the Four Seasons (No. 4607).

Arkeoloji Müzesi   Archaeological Museum

Gülhane
Parkı

Tiled Pavilion
Çinili Köşk

Museum of the Ancient Orient
Eski Şark Eserleri Müzesi

Room 3:
The Sidamara Room, named after the magnificent Sidamara Sarcophagus (No. 1179), the most beautifully decorated sarcophagus in the whole collection, found at Konya in 1950.

Rooms 4 and 5:
Not open to the public.

Room 6:
Sarcophagi from the necropolis of Sidon, including the Sarcophagus of Phaedra and Hippolytus (No. 508) and the beautiful Meleager Sarcophagus (No. 2100).

Room 7:
Sarcophagi from the Sidon necropolis (Late Roman period).

Room 8:
The world-famous Alexander Sarcophagus (No. 370), found at Sidon by Osman Hamdi Bey in 1887, so called because of its reliefs depicting Alexander the Great (scenes of hunting and battle); the Sarcophagus of the Mourners (No. 368; 4th c. B.C.) and other sarcophagi from Sidon. Bronze bust of the painter and archaeologist Osman Hamdi Bey.

Room 9:
Sarcophagus of the Satrap (No. 367; 5th c. B.C.?); Lycian Sarcophagus (No. 369; 4th c. B.C.); Tabnit Sarcophagus (No. 800; 6th c. B.C.), which originally contained the mummy of Pharaoh Eshmunazar II's father, now shown separately.

Room 10:
Finike (Phoenicia) Room, with sarcophagi (4th and 5th c. B.C.) and stelae from Sidon and other places on the Eastern Mediterranean coasts.

Room 11:
Archaic sculpture, including a stela from Bandırma (No. 1502; 5th c. B.C.) and a figure of Apollo (No. 1645; 6th c. B.C.) from the island of Samos.

Room 12:
Assos Room: fragments from the Temple of Athena (Nos. 257–268; 6th c. B.C.) at Assos, the only Doric temple in Asia Minor; colossal statue of Bes, the Cypriot Hercules (No. 3317; 6th c. B.C.).

Room 13:
Attic sculpture of the 4th and 5th c. B.C., including a figure of Athena from Trablus (No. 435) and a herm (stela representing the god Hermes; No. 1427).

Room 14:
Philiscus Room, with works by the famous Rhodian sculptor (3rd c. B.C.), including a figure of Apollo playing the lyre (No. 2000).

Room 15:
Room of the Ephebe: the famous Ephebe of Tralles (No. 1191; 3rd c. B.C.); head of Alexander the Great (No. 1138; 3rd c. B.C.; copy of an original by Lysippus); Hermaphrodite (No. 363;

3rd c. B.C.) from Pergamon; Zeus (No. 685; 3rd–2nd c. B.C.) from Troy; Euripides (No. 1242).

Room 16:
Attis Room: statue of Attis, the Phrygian god of fertility (No. 3302); stela of a warrior (No. 3980) from Kadıköy; statue of a girl (No. 2645; 2nd c. B.C.) from Antioch.

Room 17:
Aphrodisias Room: capitals, reliefs and other works of art from the city of Aphrodisias in Asia Minor (Nos. 2270–2279; 2nd c. B.C.); colossal statue of the river god Caystrus (No. 4281) from Ephesus; statue of Tyche (No. 4410; 2nd c. B.C.); Leda with the swan (No. 1494).

Room 18:
Roman Room: head of the Emperor Arcadius (No. 5028; c. A.D. 400) found in the Beyazit Meydanı in Istanbul; portrait busts of Augustus (No. 27), Tiberius (No. 385), Nero (No. 506), Hadrian (No. 50) and other emperors; statues of various divinities and mythological figures.

Room 19:
Christian art: antiquities from Byzantine Constantinople and the medieval Genoese suburb of Galata, including the Sarıgüzel Sarcophagus (No. 4508; 5th c. A.D.), the Stela of Kefalo (No. 775) and a number of tombstones dated 1347, when the Black Death struck Constantinople.

Room 20:
Byzantine art: remains of the monument of the charioteer Porphyrius (Nos. 2995 and 5560) set up in the Hippodrome by the Emperor Anastasius; Orpheus mosaic (No. 1642; 5th–6th c.) from Jerusalem; Apostle Sarcophagus (No. 5423; 5th c.) from Instanbul.

Çinili Köşk (Tiled Pavilion)   D8

Location
See plan, p. 32

Admission charge

Charge for photography

The Çinili Köşk was built by Mehmet the Conqueror, outside the palace, in 1472. It takes its name from the mosaic and the green and blue tiles with which its walls were originally clad. The ground-plan, ornament and certain other details of this two-storey columned hall show Seljuk and Persian influences.

Room 1:
Seljuk ceramics (12th–14th c.); semi-faience; glazed tiles.

Central hall:
Mihrab from İbrahim Bey Camii in Karaman (Central Anatolia); two lunette panels (16th c.; *cuerda seca* technique) from the medrese of Haseki Hürrem Camii, Istanbul.

Room 2:
Faience of the 14th and 15th c. (Seljuk and Ottoman styles).

Room 3:
İznik faience of the 16th and 17th c. Baroque fountain (partly painted, partly tiled).

Room 4:
İznik faience of the 16th and 17th c.; candlesticks from Sokullu
Mehmet Paşa Mosque (16th c.)

Room 5:
18th c. ceramics.

Room 6:
Ware from the Çanakkale manufactory (seascapes); 19th c.
ceramics.

**Eski Şark Eserleri Müzesi (Museum of the Ancient Orient)   D8

The Museum of the Ancient Orient, a branch of the
Archaeological Museum, occupies a building erected in 1883
which originally housed the Academy of Art. After reconstruction lasting many years and a complete rearrangement of the
exhibits the museum was reopened in 1974.
Only a selection of the most notable objects in the museum can
be mentioned here:
Flanking the entrance are two Hittite lions of the 14th c. B.C.

Location
See plan, p. 32

Admission charge

Charge for photography

Room 1:
Objects of the pre-Islamic period from the Arabian Peninsula:
figures, sandstone statues, tombstones, etc., including a
magnificent relief (No. 7611) with a floral design and animals'
heads and a sundial of red sandstone with an Aramaic
inscription (No. 7664).

Room 2:
Ancient Egypt (from the First Dynasty to the beginning of the
Ptolemaic Dynasty): granite sphinx (No. 10929); stela (No.
10924) with an inscription recording a victory by Pharaoh
Sethos I and a relief of Sethos offering gifts to Amon and Mut;
mummy-cases (Nos. 10891 and 10892); grave goods and
statuettes.

Room 3:
Babylonia: tile panels of the time of Nebuchadnezzar II with
figures of lions and mythological beasts. These once lined the
processional way to Babylon's Ishtar Gate (now in the
Pergamon Museum in East Berlin).
Finds from Mesopotamia: Halaf culture (5th millenium B.C.).
Old Sumerian period (transition from 4th to 3rd millennium
B.C.), Niniveh (5th period, 3rd millennium B.C.).

Room 4:
Finds from Mesopotamia and Urartu. Case 5: statuette of the
Sumerian King Lugaldalu (c. 2500 B.C.). Case 8: material from
Akkad, including tiles with cuneiform inscriptions (3rd
millenium B.C.), the oldest known examples of writing. Case 9:
material of the New Sumerian period (3rd millennium B.C.),
including a statue of King Gudea. Of particular interest is a
representation of Mesopotamian cosmology (No. 5555). Case
10: objects of the Old Babylonian period, including a diorite
statue (No. 7183; c. 2000 B.C.; head copied from original in East
Berlin) probably representing Puzur Ishtar, Governor of Mari.
Cases 11 and 12: material from Assyria.

Room 5:
New Assyrian period. In the centre of the room is a marble statue (No. 1326; 8th c. B.C.) erected in honour of a dignitary who was Chief Minister to Shalmanasar IV and Tiglath-Pileser III. Cases 14 and 15: the famous Code of Hammurabi (No. Ni 2358), the oldest code of law in the world (18th c.), and the earliest systematic astronomical observations (No. U 93103).

Room 6:
Various cultures: altar and pavement mosaic (Nos. 7760 and 7761; 7th c. B.C.) from a temple at Toprakkale (eastern Anatolia).

Passage between Rooms 6 and 7:
Material from ancient Anatolia, particularly the Hatti culture, which had its heyday in the 3rd and 2nd millenia B.C.

Room 7:
Hatti and Hittite material. In case 20 is the museum's most historic item, a clay tablet recording the Treaty of Kadesh between Pharaoh Rameses II and the Hittite King Hattusilas, the oldest known document of its kind (1269 B.C.).

Room 8:
Ancient Anatolia and the Hittites: relief from Ivriz Kaya (No. 7869); basalt lion (No. 7699; 8th c. B.C.) from the Hittite palace at Maraş; basalt sphinxes (No. 7731; 9th c. B.C.) from palace at Zincirli; torso of the Hittite King Halparundu II (No. 7772; 9th c. B.C.).

Room 9:
Basalt stela (No. 7786) with relief of a Hittite warrior; fragments of a stela of the 9th c. B.C. (No. 7754).

---

*Askeri Müzesi (Military Museum)   A9

Location
Sport ve Sergi Sarayı Çarşısı, Harbiye

Bus stop
Harbiye

Opening times
Wed.–Sun. 9 a.m.–5 p.m.
Military music 3–4 p.m.

The Military Museum, in the old Military Academy, was opened in 1959. It contains documents, arms and military equipment from the 12th c. to the present day.

12th and 13th c.:
Weapons; helmets (including an Imperial helmet).

14th c.:
Weapons of the Early Ottoman period; the helmet of Orhan Gazi; the shield of Yakup Çelebi; the armour of Gazi Evrenos Bey; equipment of the earliest military bands.

15th c.:
Paintings of the Turkish Siege of Constantinople; part of a chain with which boats were dragged over land into the Golden Horn during the final siege of Constantinople; Mameluke equipment.

16th c.:
Horse armour; spears, swords, shields, standards, helmets and other weapons, mainly of the time of Süleyman the Magnificent.

17th c.:
Bows; arrows; firearms; the sword of Sultan Mehmet IV;
manuscripts of the Koran; paintings (including a picture of the
Second Siege of Vienna).

18th and 19th c.:
Guns and pistols; flags and standards; clothing of the
Janissaries and members of the New Order; other uniforms;
pictures of the Russo-Turkish War; tents; gifts presented to
Sultan Abdül Hamid II by European States.

20th c.:
Material of the period of the Wars of Liberation and the
foundation of the Republic, including the sabre of the Greek
General Trikopis; weapons and medals of the Korean War.

Atatürk Köprüsü (Atatürk Bridge) {C6}

The Atatürk Bridge was built in its present form as a pontoon
bridge in 1935–40, replacing an earlier bridge of 1912.
The first bridge over the Golden Horn (see Haliç) was built here
in 1836 – made necessary by the extension of the city and the
economic expansion, centred on the natural harbour, which
was already taking place.

Location
Unkapanı – Azakapı

Bus stop
Unkapanı

Atatürk Kültür Sarayı (Opera House)

See Taksim Meydanı

*Atatürk Müzesi (Atatürk Museum; Museum of the Revolution) {A9}

After his return from the Syrian front in 1918 Atatürk settled
with his mother and sister in this three-storey house in Şişli.
Here he held conferences and secret meetings, before leaving
the occupied city of Istanbul in 1919 for Samsun. In 1842
the municipality acquired the house and made it an Atatürk
memorial.
In the entrance hall are displayed important speeches by the
"Father of modern Turkey". The dining-room contains pictures
of the Turkish fight for freedom, and the living-rooms have
photographs of Atatürk's life. On the first floor are personal
effects, clothing, photographs and documents, and on the
second floor a further display of important documents and
information.

Location
Halâskargazi Cad., Şişli

Bus stop
Şişli

Opening times
Daily (except 15th of
month) 9 a.m.–noon and
1–5 p.m.

Atik Ali Paşa Camii (Ali Paşa Mosque) {D7}

This mosque, situated opposite the Burned Column (see
Çemberlitaş), was founded at the end of the 15th c. by Sultan
Beyazit II's Grand Vizier, Hadım Ali Paşa. It has a T-shaped
ground-plan. The main dome is supported by eight striking
buttresses. The fountain dates from 1754.

Location
Yeniçeriler Cad.

Bus stop
Çemberlitaş

At Meydanı (Horse Square; the ancient Hippodrome) E7/8

Location
Sultanahmet

Bus stop
Sultanahmet

At Meydanı, a long square laid out in gardens, extends along the north-west side of the Blue Mosque (see Sultan Ahmet Camii). This was the site of the Roman Hippodrome, built by Septimius Severus in the 2nd c. and later enlarged by Constantine the Great.

In Byzantine times this was the centre of public life. It was the scene of chariot-races, games and mock battles; and here, too, started major political disturbances such as the Nika Insurrection of 532 which cost at least 30,000 lives. Under the Latin Emperors the Hippodrome was used for knightly tournaments; and in Palaeologue times it was again the scene of great public occasions. To the Turks occupying Constantinople in the 15th c. it served as a quarry of material for their new buildings (e.g. see Topkapı Sarayı). In the 17th c. it was the scene of great festivities and the place of execution of criminals and of State officials who had fallen into disfavour.

The Hippodrome in antiquity

The Hippodrome, oriented from south-west to north-east, was some 430 m (470 yd) long and 120 m (130 yd) across, with seating for over 30,000 spectators. Along the sides extended tiers of benches, partly of marble. At the south-west end was the *sphendone*, a semicircular structure (remains of massive foundations still visible), at the north-east end an imposing gate. On the tower on the north front there stood the four bronze horses (now replaced by copies) which Doge Enrico Dandolo carried off to Venice in 1204 (originals now in Museo Marciano; copies on gallery of San Marco). On the south-east

The German Fountain

Egyptian Obelisk

Serpent Column

side of the Hippodrome, halfway along, there probably stood the Kathisma, a structure containing the Imperial box which was directly linked with the Imperial Palace.

Alman Çeşmesi (German Fountain; Fountain of the Emperor William II)   E8

At the north-east end of At Meydanı is an octagonal fountain-house (designed by Spitta) presented by the German Emperor, William II, who visited Istanbul in 1898. Under the dome, which is decorated with mosaics and the monograms of William II and Sultan Abdül Hamid II and is borne on polished black columns, can be seen a large circular water-tank with taps at regular intervals round the outside.

Dikilitaş (Egyptian obelisk)

This granite obelisk, the upper part of an obelisk set up at Karnak in the reign of Pharaoh Tuthmosis III, was erected on the spina (the central spine) of the Hippodrome in the time of Theodosius I. The obelisk, almost 20 m (65 ft) high, stands on four copper blocks resting on a two-stage marble base, decorated on all four sides with reliefs showing Theodosius and his family in their box in the Hippodrome. On the north-east side the Emperor is seen presiding at the erection of the obelisk; on the south-east side he is presenting the victor's laurel wreath; on the south-west side he is watching a chariot-race; and on the north-west side he is accepting the submission of defeated enemies. Greek and Latin inscriptions glorify Theodosius and his prefect Proculus.

*Burmalı Sütun (Serpent Column)   E7

The Serpent Column originally stood in front of the Temple of
Apollo at Delphi, set up there in 479 B.C. by 31 Greek cities to
commemorate their victory over the Persians at Plataea. In the
time of Constantine the Great it was brought to Constantinople, where it was probably first set up in front of Haghia
Sophia and some time later moved to the Hippodrome. Of the
original structure, which must have been of imposing height,
there survives only the middle section, which consists of three
intertwined bronze snakes. On the lower coils can be seen the
names of the cities which took part in the struggle against the
Persians. The projecting snakes' heads which served as
fountains disappeared in the 17th c. One of the heads,
rediscovered in front of Ayasofya (see entry) in the 19th c., is
now in the Arkeoloji Müzesi (see entry).

Örmetaş (Mortar-Built Column)   E7

The original date of this obelisk at the south-west end of At
Meydanı, built of limestone blocks and standing 32 m (105 ft)
high, is uncertain. On the east side of the marble base is an
inscription in which the Emperor Constantine VII Por-
phyrogenitus takes credit for renovating the column, which he
compares with the Colossus of Rhodes, in honour of his
grandfather Basil I. The gilt-bronze sheets with which the
obelisk was faced were probably removed in the time of the
Crusades.

Palace of İbrahim Paşa   E7

Along the south-west side of the Hippodrome, partly
concealed under a 19th c. building, is the Palace of İbrahim
Paşa, a Greek who became Grand Vizier in the time of
Süleyman the Magnificent. The palace, completed in 1524,
was the largest private residence ever built in the Ottoman
Empire. After İbrahim's murder in 1536 his whole property
passed into the hands of the State and was converted to a great
variety of purposes. His once-magnificent mansion, much
dilapidated in the course of time, is now being restored for use
as a museum.

Palace of Antiochus, St Euphemia's Church and
Palace of Lausus   E7/8

Location
NW of Hippodrome

North-west of the Hippodrome, between Adalet Sarayı (Law
Courts) and the Firuz Ağa Mosque, are the excavated remains
of three monumental Byzantine buildings.
On the north-east side of the Law Courts are the remains of the
Palace of Antiochus, built in the 5th c. by a high dignitary at the
Court of Theodosius II. After the repression of the Nika
Insurrection the central part of the palace was converted into a
church dedicated to St Euphemia.
Near the Firuz Ağa Mosque are the remains of the Palace of
Lausus, built by another high official of the 5th c.

*Aya İrini Kilisesi (Church of Haghia Eirene) D8

The Church of Haghia Eirene (Church of the Divine Peace) is one of the best-preserved Byzantine buildings in Istanbul. Probably built about 300 on the site of a Temple of Aphrodite, it was an episcopal church in pre-Constantinian times. The Second Ecumenical Council met here in 381. The church was several times rebuilt after suffering destruction by fire or earthquake. It was used by the Turks as an arsenal; thereafter, until 1826, it housed a collection of antiquities and weapons. The church now has the status of a museum, and is used from time to time as an impressive setting for concerts.

Location
SW side of Outer Court of
Topkapı Sarayı

Bus stops
Gülhane Parkı, Sultanahmet

Opening times
Daily (except 5th of month)
9 a.m.–5 p.m.

The oldest visible parts of the church, a three-aisled basilica with two domes, date from the 6th c. The aisles are separated from one another by colonnades and by the massive piers supporting the dome. The galleries appear to have been an 8th c. innovation; unlike the lower part of the church, there is no separation here between the nave and the side aisles. The apse is also an interesting feature, with its three large windows and five tiers of seating round the curved end. Five doorways lead into the narthex and, beyond this, the remains of the atrium of Justinian's time.

Architecture

In the domed apse are the remains of a mosaic depicting a cross on a gold ground. There are also fragments of mosaics in the main dome, on the walls and in the narthex.

Mosaics

Church of Haghia Eirene

Ayasofya (Haghia Sophia)   D/E8

Location Ayasofya Meydanı
Bus stop Sultanahmet
Admission charge
Charge for photography

History

Haghia Sophia, the Church of the Divine Wisdom, is one of the wonders of the world. For almost a thousand years it was the spiritual centre of the Byzantine Empire. After the fall of Constantinople to the Turks it became the principal mosque of Istanbul; and since 1935 it has been a museum – one of the world's most visited museums.

The first church on this site was founded by Constantine the Great in 326. At first known merely as the Great Church (Megale Ekklesia), it was later named the Church of the Divine Wisdom (Haghia Sophia). In 404 this church was burned down. In the reign of Theodosius II it was replaced by a five-aisled church, which in turn was destroyed in 532 during the Nika Insurrection. Thereupon Justinian I summoned Anthemius of Tralles and Isidore of Miletus to build the most splendid place of worship of antiquity. Twenty years later Haghia Sophia suffered damage in an earthquake, and after the repair of the damage was solemnly reconsecrated in 563.

Subsequently it was restored on several occasions. In 1317, during the reign of the Emperor Andronicus Palaeologus, the structure was strengthened by the addition of rather unsightly buttresses. In the Ottoman period, when the church became a mosque, the four minarets at the corners of the building were added. In 1847–49 the building was thoroughly restored by the Fossati brothers at the behest of Sultan Abdül Mecit, bringing to light some of the mosaics which had been covered with whitewash by the Turks. Since 1935, when Haghia Sophia

Ayasofya (Haghia Sophia)

Section

Ayasofya

Plan

Haghia Sophia

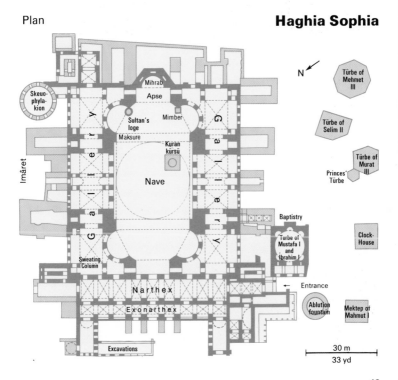

N

Türbe of Mehmet III

Türbe of Selim II

Türbe of Murat III

Princes' Türbe

Clock-House

Skeuo-phyla-kion

Imâret

Mihrab
Apse
Sultan's loge
Mimber
Maksure
Kuran kürsü

G a l l e r y

G a l l e r y

Nave

Sweating Column

Baptistry

Türbe of Mustafa I and İbrahim I

Entrance

N a r t h e x

E x o n a r t h e x

Ablution fountain

Mektep of Mahmut I

Excavations

30 m
33 yd

43

Haghia Sophia: Turkish plaques on the main piers

became a museum, further mosaics have been exposed. Outside the west front, too, remains of the pre-Justinianic building have been discovered.

Architecture

Haghia Sophia is a domed basilica, with a nave flanked by two lateral aisles on either side. At the east end is the apse (now the mihrab). At the west end are the inner and the outer narthex (exonarthex). The church is over 100 m (330 ft) long; the nave is 32·3 m (106 ft) wide. The shallow dome (height 55·6 m (182 ft), diameter 31 m (102 ft), no longer exactly circular as a result of repair work, is surrounded by six small and two large semi-domes. The buttresses and supports added to the original building, together with the associated Turkish structures (medrese, türbes) increase the impression of solidity of a building which is sufficiently massive in itself.

Entrance

The original entrance was in the west front, where recent investigations have pointed to the existence of a colonnaded forecourt. In the course of time, however, the entrance was moved to the south end of the narthex. The ancient bronze door gives access to the vestibule, with the beautiful mosaics, rediscovered only in 1933, of the Mother of God enthroned with the Christ Child and the Emperors Constantine the Great (on right, holding a model of a walled town representing Constantinople) and Justinian (on left, with a model of Haghia Sophia).

Narthex

The long narrow narthex is spanned by nine arches. Five doorways on the left give access to the exonarthex, nine doorways on the right lead into the nave. Above the

Haghia Sophia: Christ with Constantine IX and Zoe

monumental central doorway into the nave, the Imperial Doorway, is a mosaic depicting Christ enthroned, his right hand raised in blessing, his left hand holding a book with the inscription "Peace be with you: I am the light of the world." At Christ's feet is the kneeling figure of the Emperor Leo IV, indicating that the mosaic dates from his reign.

Nave

The nave is dominated by the central dome, which, in the flood of light admitted by its 40 windows, seems to float in the air over the four massive piers which support it. On the east and west sides of the main dome are two semi-domes, broken up by three semicircular niches, the central niche on the east side being enlarged to form the principal apse. The eight dark green monolithic columns in the nave, four on each side between the main piers, are believed to have come from some earlier building. The others are from stone quarries in Thessaly and marble quarries on the island of Proconnesus in the Sea of Marmara. The pavement and the frames of the doors and windows are also of Proconnesian marble. The walls up to the springing of the arches are faced with variously coloured and patterned marble panels separated by narrow strips of porphyry and bands of foliage ornament, the veining of adjacent panels being symmetrically arranged.

The marble pavement is structured by strips of verd antique. The *opus alexandrinum* (with panels of differently coloured granite, porphyry and verd antique) at the south-east corner of the nave is particularly fine: according to an account by the Archbishop of Novgorod in 1200, this was the position of the Imperial Throne.

The capitals of the columns are notable for the beauty of their forms and their leaf patterns: Byzantine developments of an earlier type.

In the semi-dome of the choir apse is the Mother of God enthroned with the Child. At the base of the arch framing the apse, on the south side, is a figure of the Archangel Michael with brilliantly gleaming wings; opposite, on the north side, are the remains of a mosaic of the Archangel Gabriel.

From the nave three other mosaics can be seen in the niches of the north tympanum. They represent the three sainted bishops of the young church – St Ignatius the Younger (first niche from the west), St John Chrysostum (central niche) and St Ignatius Theophorus (fifth niche from west). All three wear the omophorion with the characteristic three crosses.

In the pendentives on the east side of the dome are six-winged seraphim and cherubim; in those on the west side are imitations dating from the restoration by the Fossati brothers.

Gallery

According to an old tradition the whole of the gallery was originally the gynaeceum (the women's part of the church). Parts of the south gallery were reserved for the Imperial Family. Church Councils were sometimes held here.

Above the northern gallery is a mosaic of the Emperor Alexander (10th c.). The representation of the magnificent Imperial coronet is particularly fine.

In the south gallery is a mosaic of the Deesis, one of the finest 14th c. works of its kind. It shows Christ with his hand raised in blessing, flanked by the Virgin and John the Baptist interceding for mankind. Set in the pavement opposite the Deesis is the tombstone of Doge Enrico Dandolo, one of the leaders of the Fourth Crusade. At the east end of the south gallery, near the apse, is a mosaic of Christ enthroned, flanked by Empress Zoe and her third husband Constantine IX Monomachus in the ceremonial act of making an offering. Adjoining is a mosaic depicting Emperor John II Comnenus, his wife Irene (daughter of King Ladislaus of Hungary) and their son Alexius making an offering to the Virgin and Child.

Turkish furnishings

In the apse is the mihrab, which indicates the direction of Mecca. On the four main piers are huge circular wooden plaques inscribed in gold script with the names of the first four Caliphs (Abu Bekr, Omar, Osman and Ali), which disturb the harmonious proportions of the interior. Against the piers of the apse, borne on antique columns, are the octagonal Sultan's loge, enclosed by a screen (left), and the mimber or Friday pulpit (right). Opposite, on the north-east pier, is the maksure. Between the two southern piers is the Koran-reader's platform. The two 2 m (6½ ft) high alabaster urns at the entrance to the mosque are said to have been put there by Sultan Murat III. Halfway along the south aisle is a niche for the Koran, with a fine metal grille and deep blue tiles. The library, which is entered from here, also has beautiful tiles.

Sweating Column

At the north-west corner of the north aisle is the legendary Sweating Column, which always feels damp and has been credited since time immemorial with miraculous healing qualities.

◀ *Haghia Sophia: the nave*

Ayasofya

Skeuophylakion

The Skeuophylakion, a circular room at the north-east corner of the church, originally housed the church treasury. The masonry suggests that it may have been built as early as the 4th c.

Imâret

Built on to the north wall of Haghia Sophia is the Imâret, a public kitchen and dining-room built in the Turkish period.

Baptistery

The Baptistery on the south side of Haghia Sophia, on an octagonal plan with a domed roof, dates from the time of Justinian. The Turks converted it into a türbe (mausoleum), which contains the tombs of Sultans Mustafa I and İbrahim I.

Fountain

Opposite the Baptistery is the ablution fountain (c. 1740), one of the finest Rococo examples of its kind. Notable features are its widely projecting and gaily painted roof and its elegant bronze grille.

Clock-House

The Clock-House was built by the Fossati brothers in 1847–49. This was the house of the Mosque Astronomer. The old sundial can still be seen on the façade of Haghia Sophia.

Türbe of Selim II

The türbe designed by Sinan for Sultan Selim II, in the gardens in front of the mosques, is one of the largest of its kind. Architecturally it is interesting, with its square ground-plan, double dome and octagonal upper storey supported by a ring of columns. The interior is clad with beautiful Iznik tiles.

Türbe of Murat III

The Türbe of Murat III was built by Davut Paşa in 1599. It has a double dome and a hexagonal ground-plan, with an interior of beautifully patterned İznik tiles.
Built up against this türbe is the small Princes' Türbe, in which five sons of Murat IV are buried.

Türbe of Mehmet III

Adjoining the eastern wall of the gardens is the Türbe of Sultan Mehmet III, on an octagonal ground-plan.

Ayasofya Meydanı (Ayasofya Square; Forum Augusteum)   E8

Bus stop
Sultanahmet

The square on the south-west side of Haghia Sophia was in Byzantine times the Forum Augusteum, surrounded by Imperial palaces, official buildings and the Baths of Zeuxippus. On its west side was the Milion, the zero milestone from which all road distances were reckoned.
From the Forum Augusteum the Via Triumphalis (Mese; now Divan Yolu Caddesi) ran east to the Forum Tauri (see Beyazit Meydanı).

Baths of Roxelana

See Haseki Hürrem Hamamı

Azapkapı Camii (Sokullu Mehmet Paşa Camii)   C6/7

Location
N end of Atatürk Bridge,
Azapkapı

Bus stop
Azapkapı

The Azapkapı Mosque, now rather cramped by the approach to the Atatürk Bridge, was built by Sinan in 1577 for Sokullu Mehmet Paşa, a Bosnian nobleman who served three Sultans as Grand Vizier.
The mosque stands on a high basement once occupied by shops, and is square in plan, with the mihrab projecting on the

south-east side. The main dome, which is surrounded by eight semi-domes, is borne on "elephants' feet" columns.

The mihrab and mimber are of marble, beautifully worked. Some of the original tiled decoration has been lost, but the Kütahya tiles substituted in the most recent restoration are of excellent quality. An interesting architectural feature, apart from the basement storey, is the minaret, which is separate from the mosque but connected with it by an arch.

*Bab-ı ali (Sublime Porte)   D8

The famous Sublime Porte (recently restored) gives access to the former residence of the Grand Vizier of the Ottoman Empire, where all matters of high State policy were handled. Here foreign ambassadors were accredited, and here they were informed of the decisions of the Ottoman Government.

The Sublime Porte was originally built in the mid 17th c., but dates in its present form from the 19th. It has a fine curving roof in the Baroque manner.

Location
Alemdar Cad.

Bus stop
Gülhane Parkı

Balık Pazarı

See İstiklâl Caddesi

Bazaar

See Kapalı, Çarsı, Mısır Çarşısı

Bedesten

See Kapalı Çarşı

*Belediye Müzesi (Municipal Museum)   D5

The Istanbul Municipal Museum, installed in the Gazenferağa Medrese in Saraçhane in 1946, has a rich collection of material on the history of the city (pictures, plans, documents). Istanbul craft products down the centuries (glass, porcelain, bronze and copper vessels, writing equipment), furniture and domestic equipment of many periods and much else besides (including the first piano to come to Istanbul). There is also an imposing portrait of Sultan Mehmet II, the Conqueror.

Location
Atatürk Bulvarı, at Aqueduct of Valens

Bus stop
Atatürk Bulvarı

Opening times
Daily (except 5th of month)
10 a.m.–12 noon and
1.30–5 p.m.

Belediye Sarayı (Town Hall)   D5

Istanbul's Town Hall, an ultra-modern building completed some years ago, shows an unusually imaginative style which makes it more appealing than much contemporary architecture.

Location
Atatürk Bulvarı/
Şehzadebaşı Cad.

Belediye Sarayı

Istanbul Town Hall

Fishmongers in Beşiktaş

Bus stop
Belediyesi

The main elements in the structure are glass and aluminium, but the effect of the building is enhanced by arches, a finely contrived projecting bay and the attractively laid out gardens, with flower-beds, fountains and bronze busts of mayors of Istanbul.

Belgrat Ormanı (Belgrade Forest)

Location
20 km (12½ miles) N of city centre

To the north of Istanbul extends the Belgrade Forest, an area of great importance for the city's water-supply. This wooded and well-watered region, broken up by gullies, is now a popular recreation area. The forest is named after a settlement established in the time of Süleyman the Magnificent to house workers brought in from Belgrade to maintain the water channels and reservoirs and tend the forest. A number of reservoirs and aqueducts dating from Byzantine times were reactivated in the 16th c. by Sinan, the famous Court Architect, and incorporated in a well-designed water-supply system. The inhabitants of Belgrat were moved out at the end of the 19th c. and the village itself left to decay. The city still draws much of its water from installations in the Belgrade Forest.

Beşiktaş A/B10–12

Location
European shore of Bosphorus

The district of Beşiktaş on the European side of the Bosphorus, like other settlements on the Bosphorus, originated as a Greek colony. In Byzantine times Beşiktaş had a large church, a busy harbour, a hippodrome and an Imperial summer palace; but of all these buildings practically nothing is left.

At the landing-stage of this lively Istanbul suburb is a prominent memorial (by Zühtü Müridoğlu, 1946) to the celebrated Ottoman admiral Hayrettin Paşa (Barbarossa). Facing the monument is the octagonal Türbe of Heyrettin Paşa, one of Sinan's earliest works. At the corner of Beşiktaş Caddesi and Barbaros Bulvarı is the Sinan Paşa Mosque (1556), which closely resembles the Üç Şerefeli Mosque in Edirne (see entry).

Bus stop
Beşiktaş

Boat landing-stage
Beşiktaş

See Deniz Müzesi

Maritime Museum

See Dolmabahçe Sarayı

Dolmabahçe Palace

See Resim ve Heykel Müzesi

Museum of Modern Art

---

*Beyazit Camii (Beyazit Mosque)   D6

This mosque, designed by Hayrettin, was built for Sultan Beyazit II, son of Mehmet the Conqueror, in the first decade of the 16th c. Its architecture resembles that of the Yeşil Camii in Bursa (see entry), but already shows features characteristic of the transition to the Classical style. The main dome, pierced by 34 windows, is borne on four marble "elephants' feet" and two porphyry columns and is supported by two large semi-domes (one on the side towards the entrance, the other on the mihrab

Location
Beyazit Meydanı

Bus stop
Beyazit

Landing-stage, Beşiktaş

side), with four smaller domes along the north-east and south-west sides. The two minarets give the mosque its distinctive character. The interior is notable for the beautiful decoration of the domes. Also very fine are the marble Sultan's loge and the mihrab, with inscriptions by the celebrated calligrapher Şeyh Hamdullah.

The garden court, surrounded by 24 domes, is one of the most beautiful of its kind in Istanbul, with three handsome doorways and a finely carved ablution fountain.

The subsidiary buildings associated with the mosque (caravanserai, public kitchen, medrese and primary school) now house the Beyazit State Library (which incorporates the Veliyüddin Efendi Library, founded in 1736), the Municipal Library and the Hakki-tarik-us Library. Outside the mihrab are the Türbe of Sultan Beyazit II, erected by Selim I, and two other tombs.

Beyazit Kulesi (Beyazit Tower)

See Üniversite

Beyazit Meydanı (Beyazit Square)   D6

Bus stop
Beyazit

This square, now named after the Beyazit Mosque, occupies much of the area of the Forum Tauri of Byzantine times. It is bounded on the north by the Moorish gateway of the University (see Üniversite), and on its south side is the Simkeş Han, within the precincts of which remains of the Theodosian Triumphal Arch (4th c.) were recently discovered.

---

*Beylerbeyi

Beylerbey Camii (Beylerbey Mosque)

Location
Asiatic shore of Bosphorus

Bus stop
Beylerbeyi

Boat landing-stage
Beylerbeyi

The Beylerbey Mosque was built by Mehmet Tahir Ağa in 1778 for Sultan Abdül Hamit I. Originally it had only a minaret, but a medrese and a hamam were later added. In 1820, during the reign of Sultan Mahmut II, it was thoroughly restored and provided with a lodge for the Padishah, a clock-room and a second minaret.

The tiles in the interior are of different periods. The mimber, Kuran kürsü and screen doors are of walnut wood, with very fine ivory intarsia work.

Beylerbey Sarayı (Beylerbey Palace)

The Baylerbey Palace, picturesquely situated on the eastern shore of the Bosphorus, was built by Sarkis Balyan in 1865, in a style very similar to the Dolmabahçe Palace (see entry). It was mainly used for the accommodation of foreign heads of State and other distinguished visitors. Sultan Abdül Hamit spent his last years here after his return from exile in 1913.

The effect of the palace is enhanced by the two marble pavilions at the ends of the waterfront and the beautifully laid out gardens.

See Boğaziçi Köprüsü

Bosphorus Bridge

Beyoğlu (previously known as Pera)   B/C7/8

The higher ground above Galata is occupied by the district of Beyoğlu, known in Ottoman times as Pera. This was the area favoured for the embassies of foreign Powers and the residences of wealthy merchants. Some remains of former splendour can still be seen along what was once its grand main street, the Grande Rue de Péra (see İstiklâl Caddesi). After the foundation of the Turkish Republic, and particularly after the Second World War, the commercial centre drifted farther north along Cumhuriyet Caddesi (see entry). As a result the best and most exclusive shopping streets in Istanbul are now to be found in the Şişli and Osmanbey districts, north of Beyoğlu.

Location
Between Tünel Meydanı and Taksim Meydanı

Bus stops
Taksim, Galatasaray, Tünel

See İstiklâl Caddesi

Independence Street

See Taksim Meydanı

Taksim Square

Binbirdirek (1001 Columns)   E7

The Binbirdirek Cistern is the second largest of the covered cisterns of Istanbul, with a capacity of some 50,000 cu. m (1·1 million gallons). Like Yerebatan Sarayı (see entry), the largest, it was constructed in the 6th c. It is 64 m (210 ft) long by 56 m (184 ft) wide. The roof is supported by 224 columns 12·5 m (41 ft) high set in 16 rows at intervals of about 4 m (13 ft) and linked by stone ties. The effect is one of immense space.

Location
Near Divan Yolu

Bus stop
Beyazit

Blachernae Palace

See Tekfur Sarayı

Black Sea

See Kara Deniz

Blue Mosque

See Sultan Ahmet Camii

Bodrum Camii (Bodrum Mosque; Myrelaion)   E5

Location
Lâleli Cad., Aksaray

Bus stop
Lâleli

The Bodrum Camii was originally a church belonging to the Monastery of the Myrelaion, founded by the Emperor Romanus Lecapenus next to his palace. It was converted into a mosque in the time of Sultan Beyazit II. This 10th c. domed church stands on an unusual substructure (Turkish bodrum=cellar), probably designed as a crypt for members of the Imperial Family. The building was badly damaged by fire in the 13th c. and again in 1911.

Adjoining the mosque are remains of the Byzantine palace.

**Boğaziçi (Bosphorus)   A–E9–12

The Bosphorus (Ford of the Cow), known in Turkish as Boğaziçi (the Strait), is a former river valley which was drowned by the sea at the end of the Tertiary period. Some 32 km (20 miles) long and up to 3·3 km (2 miles) wide, ranging in depth from 30 m (100 ft) to 120 m (395 ft), it extends from the Black Sea to the Sea of Marmara and, together with the Dardanelles, separates Europe from Asia. With its shores rising to heights of up to 200 m (650 ft), lined with palaces, ruins, villages and gardens, it is one of the most beautiful stretches of scenery in Turkey.

By boat along the Bosphorus

The best way of seeing the Bosphorus in all its beauty is to take a trip on one of the coastal boats which ply along its length, calling in alternately at landing-stages on each side and thus affording a constantly changing panorama. The point of departure is just south-east of the Galata Bridge; the ports of call can be seen in the timetables displayed in the waiting-room. Not all boats go as far as Rumeli Kavağı, the last station on the European side (1¾–2 hours). At each station there is a ferry to the other side.

European side

	Istanbul
Dolmabahçe	See Dolmabahçe Sarayı
Çırağan	See Çırağan Sarayı
Yıldız Park	See entry
Bosphorus Bridge	See Boğaziçi Köprüsü
Kuruçeşme	The boat sails past the little promontory of Defterdar Burun and Duimi Bank (navigational light) to the village of Kuruçeşme and the little fishing hamlet of Arnavutköy on Akıntı Point, where there is always a strong current.
Bebek	Bebek, in a beautiful bay, with villas and country houses (*yalılar*).
Rumeli Hisarı	See entry

A yalı on the Bosphorus

See entry	Emirgân
İstinye, with a shipyard.	İstinye
Yeniköy (last station for most boats), with beautiful villas and gardens. In St George's Church is an old icon of the Mother of God Kamariotissa.	Yeniköy
Tarabya (Therapia), a sizeable township in a little bay, known in antiquity as Pharmakeios (Poisoner, after the poison strewn here by Medea in her pursuit of Jason). Pleasantly cool in summer thanks to the wind blowing in from the Black Sea. Tarabya has numbers of elegant country houses, where some of the European diplomatic missions take up their summer quarters.	Tarabya
From this little cape the Black Sea can be seen in the distance, to the right.	Cape Kireç
Büyükdere is a popular summer resort, with a large park. The bay of Büyükdere (= large valley) forms the broadest part of the Bosphorus (3·3 km (2 miles)). Inland, 10 km (6 miles) north-west, is the Belgrade Forest (see Belgrat Ormanı).	Büyükdere
Sarıyer, at the mouth of the wooded and well-watered Valley of Roses. There is an interesting museum, Sadberk Koç Hanım Müzesi (tiles, porcelain, glass, crystal, silver, costumes, jewellery; documents relating to the Sadberk Koç family), opened in 1981 in the old Azaryan Yalı. From Sarıyer a bus or dolmuş can be taken to the little Black Sea resort of Kilyos,	Sarıyer

Holiday resort on the Bosphorus

10 km (6 miles) north, which has a good sandy beach. Then on past the Dikili cliffs.

Rumeli Kavağı

Rumeli Kavağı, the last station on the European side, lies below a castle built by Murat IV in 1628. On a hill to the north are the ruins of the Byzantine Castle of Imroz Kalesi, the walls of which once reached right down to the sea and were continued by a mole, which could be linked by a chain with the mole and the walls of Yoroz Kalesi on the Asiatic side.

Altın Kum

In summer the boats usually go on to the nearby resort of Altın Kum (Golden Sand), with a restaurant on the plateau (views) enclosed by an old fortification.

North end of Bosphorus

The tourist ships continue to the north end of the Bosphorus, 4·5 km (3 miles) wide, and turn back when they reach the Black Sea. On both sides bare basalt cliffs rise almost vertically from the sea.

Büyük Liman

Between Rumeli Kavağı and the Garipçe Kalesi promontory is the small Bay of Büyük Liman.

Rumeli Feneri

Rumeli Feneri (European Lighthouse), stands at the north entrance to the Bosphorus, with the village of the same name and an old fortress on the cliffs at the north end of the bay. The dark basalt cliffs to the east are the Cyanaean Islands or Symplegades (the "clashing rocks" of the Argonaut legend).

Asiatic side

Istanbul

See entry	Üsküdar
Kuzguncuk, separated from Üsküdar by a hill.	Kuzguncuk
See entry	Beylerbeyi
See Boğaziçi Köprüsü	Bosphorus Bridge
Past Çengelköy, Kuleli, Vanıköy and Top Dagı (Cannon Hill, 130 m (427 ft)), famed for its view over the whole of the Bosphorus, to Kandilli, on the promontory opposite Bebek Bay.	Top Dagı
See entry	Küçüksu
Between Kandilli and Anadolu Hisarı is the beautiful Valley of the Sweet Waters of Asia, at the mouth of the Göksu (Heavenly Water).	Mouth of the Göksu
See entry	Anadolu Hisarı
Kanlıca, on a small promontory. On the shore is the Summer Palace of Vizier Köprülü (17th c.), built on piles.	Kanlıca
Çubuklu, in Beykoz Bay. In Byzantine times there was a Monastery of the Akoimetoi (the Unsleeping Ones) here, in which the monks, in shifts, continued in prayer day and night.	Çubuklu

View across the Bosphorus

Boğaziçi

Paşabahçe

At the head of the bay is Paşabahçe, with beautiful gardens. Near the shore is a Persian-style palace built by Murat III.

Beykoz

Beykoz, at the north end of Beykoz Bay.

An hour's drive to the north is Yuşa Tepesi (Joshua's Hill, 195 m (640 ft); at present in a closed area), known to Europeans as the Giant's Grave, an important landmark for vessels coming from the Black Sea. The road runs behind the Palace of Mohammed Ali Paşa up the wooded and well-watered Valley of Hünkar İskelesi, once a favoured estate of the Byzantine Emperors and the Sultans. On the summit of the hill is a mosque, with the Giant's Grave and a view extending over the whole of the Bosphorus (though Istanbul itself is concealed) and part of the Black Sea.

Beyond the conspicuous Palace of Mohammed Ali and the mouth of the Hünkar İskelesi Valley are the Promontory of Selvi Burun and the little Bay of Umur Yeri.

Anadolu Kavağı

Anadolu Kavağı last station on the Asiatic side, is an authentically Turkish village in Macar Bay, between two promontories with abandoned forts. On the northern promontory is the picturesque ruin of the Byzantine Castle of Yoroz Kalesi, known since the 14th c. as the Genoese Castle. In antiquity the promontory and the strait (one of the narrowest points in the Bosphorus) were called Hieron (Holy Place), after the Altar of the Twelve Gods and a Temple of Zeus Urios, granter of fair winds.

Keçili Bay

Beyond Macar Bay is the wide Keçili Bay, bounded on the north by the Fil Burun Promontory.

Anadolu Feneri

Anadolu Feneri (Anatolian Lighthouse) on a low cape by the village of the same name, is situated on the cliff-fringed coast, with an old fort.

North end of Bosphorus

Then come Kabakos Bay, with basalt cliffs in which countless sea-birds nest, and the steep-sided Promontory of Yum Burun, at the northern entrance to the Bosphorus.

---

*Boğaziçi Köprüsü (Bosphorus Bridge)

Location
Ortaköy–Beylerbeyi

Bus stops
Ortaköy, Beylerbeyi

Boat landing-stage
Beylerbeyi

This suspension bridge, opened to traffic in the 50th anniversary year of the Turkish Republic (1973), has the longest span in Europe and the fourth largest in the world. It forms part of the northern ring road (of motorway standard) round Istanbul and is an essential element in the European Highway (E5) which runs from Ostend to the Middle East.

Plans to bridge the Bosphorus have had a very long history. A legendary forerunner of the present road bridge linking Europe and Asia was the bridge of boats built by Darius so that his army could cross over into Greece. During the Renaissance both Leonardo da Vinci and Michelangelo occupied themselves with the design of bridges over the Bosphorus. French engineers put forward a plan for a bridge at the end of the 19th c., but nothing came of it, nor of a later project for a tunnel between Stamboul and Üsküdar. It was only in the 1960s that serious preparations for building a bridge began to be made,

The Bosphorus Bridge

and in 1970 the construction of the present steel box-girder suspension bridge was begun by a British/German consortium.
Technical data:
total length 1560 m (1706 yd)
span between pylons 1074 m (1175 yd)
width 33·4 m (110 ft); six lanes
clearance 64 m (210 ft) above sea-level
height of pylons 165 m (541 ft)
There are plans to build a second bridge over the Bosphorus at Rumeli Hisarı in the next few years.

Bosphorus

See Boğaziçi

*Bozdoğan Kemeri (Aqueduct of Valens)   D5

The Aqueduct of Valens, part of a water-supply system constructed in the reign of the 4th c. Emperor Valens, spanned the saddle between the Third and Fourth Hills of Constantinople. Of the original length of some 1000 m (1100 yd), roughly 920 m (1000 yd) are still standing to a maximum height of 26·5 m (87 ft). The aqueduct was frequently repaired in the course of its history, and at the end of the 17th c., Sultan Mustafa II had part of it restored to its original condition.

Location
Atatürk Bulvarı

Bus stop
Atatürk Bulvarı

The Aqueduct of Valens (Bozdoğan Kemeri)

Bucoleon Palace   E7/8

Location
Kennedy Cad.

The Bucoleon Palace (named after statues of an ox and a lion that stood here) was part of an Imperial palace which was probably founded in the 4th c. and enlarged in several stages, particularly during the reigns of Justinian I and Theophilus. Substantial remains of the palace, the Emperor's private harbour and a Byzantine lighthouse still survive.

Building Museum

See Amcazade Hüseyin Paşa Medresesi

Burned Column

See Çemberlitaş

* *Bursa

Situation
100 km (62 miles) S of
Istanbul as the crow flies

Bursa (known in antiquity as Prusa and later as Brusa), capital of the Ottoman Empire in its early days, lies in a fertile plain watered by the Nilüfer on a limestone terrace dissected by two mountain streams, the Gök Dere and the Djilimbos, below the north-west side of Uludağ, the Bithynian Olympus. Its altitude ranges between 150 m (490 ft) and 250 m (820 ft). The city has a population of a million (conurbation 1·2 million).

Bursa's beautiful situation, its picturesque old town and its magnificent buildings (mosques and türbes) make it one of the most attractive and interesting places in Turkey. Its thermal springs, on the north-western outskirts of the city, were much frequented in Roman times and still attract large numbers of visitors.

Access
By car or bus from Istanbul via İzmit and Yalova (235 km (146 miles)); by regular boat service from Istanbul to Yalova, then bus

Bursa's favoured climate can be judged from the following figures: mean annual temperature 14·5 °C (58·1 °F), July mean 24·2 °C (75·6 °F), October mean 20 °C (68 °F), January mean 5·2 °C (41·4 °F).

Climate

Bursa, a provincial capital and the seat of a university, has one of the most vigorous economies of any Turkish city. This is due not only to the fertile soil of the surrounding area with its flourishing agriculture (fruit and vegetable production, particularly peaches and apricots; several canning plants) but also to its large textile factories, based on an efficient silk-spinning industry. In recent years, too, many metal-processing firms have been established here.

A significant contribution to the city's economy is also made by the holiday and tourist trade, which is being promoted by the steady modernisation of the spa establishments (sulphurous and chalybeate waters) in the suburb of Çekirge.

Economy

The foundation of the town is attributed to the Bithynian King Prusias I, the date of foundation to the year 186 B.C. The earliest settlement was on the citadel hill, which was also the site of the Roman town. During the reign of Trajan the town's baths were rebuilt and a library established by Pliny the Younger, then Governor of Bithynia.

In Byzantine times the importance of the town continued to depend mainly on its medicinal springs. About 950, after several unsuccessful attacks, the Arabs captured and destroyed the town. After its reconquest by the Emperor Alexius Comnenus it fell into the hands of the Seljuks in 1097, but by the beginning of the Fourth Crusade it was again held by the Byzantines.

In 1326 Orsan, son of Osman I (the first Turkish Sultan), took the city, and it then became the first Ottoman capital (until 1361). The heyday of Bursa was in the 15th c., when it acquired numerous fine buildings and works of art. In the 19th c. it was ravaged by fires and earthquakes. In 1920 it was taken by the Greeks but was recovered by the Turks two years later.

History

Arkeoloji Müzesi (Archaeological Museum)

Originally housed in the Green Medrese. Bursa's Archaeological Museum moved in 1972 to a new building in the Çekirge Park of Culture. The new museum has four exhibition halls, store-rooms, a library and a laboratory.

Location
Çekirge Kültür Parkı

Opening times
Daily 10 a.m.–5 p.m.

Room 1:
Prehistoric figurines, pottery and stone and metal objects; Roman, Byzantine and European (15th–18th c.) coins.

Bursa

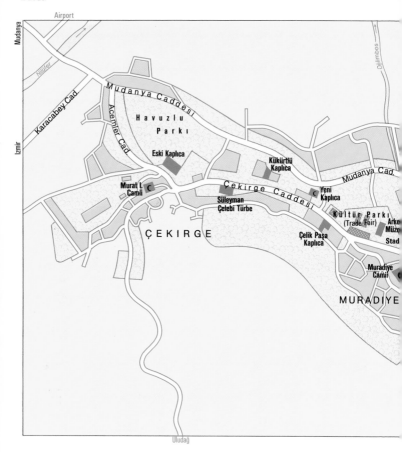

Room 2:
Archaic, Hellenistic, Roman and Byzantine vases, reliefs and inscriptions (all from Bursa and its immediate area).

Room 3:
Classical Anatolian pottery, glass and metal objects; pottery, figurines, gold and silver of the Hellenistic and Roman periods; fine Roman decorative glass.

Room 4:
Gallery of art and applied art, with special exhibitions.

Garden:
Columns, capitals, sarcophagi, funerary stelae and statues of various periods.

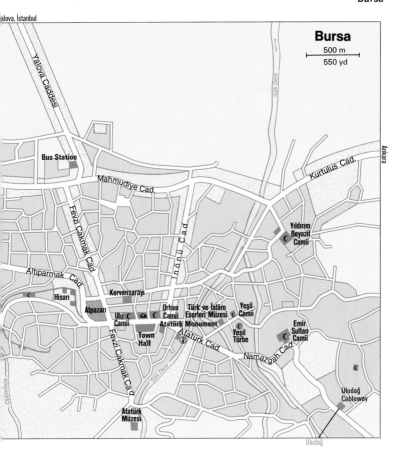

Atatürk Müzesi (Atatürk Museum)

The "Father of modern Turkey" stayed in this trim late 19th c. villa during his 13 visits to Bursa between 1923 and 1938; it became the Atatürk Museum in 1973. It contains furniture and personal effects belonging to Atatürk and a variety of documentation on his life.

Location
Çekirge

Atpazarı (Bazaar)

The Bazaar, which was badly damaged by an earthquake in 1855 and a fire in 1957, has recently been restored. Notable features are the Bedesten with its 14 domes, one of the earliest of its kind (c. 1400), and several hans (caravanserais).

Location
City centre

Türbe at Mosque of Murat II

Çekirge

Location
3 km (2 miles) W

In the suburb of Çekirge are some of the most celebrated sulphurous and chalybeate thermal springs and baths in the East. Known in antiquity as the "Royal Springs", they were undoubtedly in use before the Roman Imperial period; but both the Roman and the Byzantine buildings, which were visited by the Empress Theodora among others, have almost completely disappeared.

The Eski Kaplıca (Old Bath) was built by Sultan Murat I, using the remains of an earlier building. Close by is his first mosque, Gazi Hunkiar Camii (1365), on a cruciform plan. On the terrace of the mosque is the Türbe of Murat I, who was murdered in 1389 after the Battle of Kosovo in Serbia.

The Yeni Kaplıca (New Bath), a master work of architecture with beautiful marble and tile decoration, was built by Grand Vizier Rüstem Paşa in the 16th c.

Other well-known bath establishments are the Kara Mustafa Paşa Kaplıcası (radioactive water) and the Armutlu Kaplıca (treatment of gynaecological conditions).

Almost all the larger hotels have piped thermal water.

Hisarı (Citadel)

Location
W of city centre

The Citadel is strategically situated on a small plateau which falls steeply away on the north, east and west sides and on the south side is linked with the Uludağ Massif by a lower-lying area with numerous springs. The Citadel proper is surrounded by a wall, originally with four gates, which was built in Roman times and several times renovated during the Byzantine and Ottoman periods. Here, too, are the türbes of Sultans Orhan and Osman, which were badly damaged by an earthquake in 1855 and rebuilt in the reign of Sultan Abdül Aziz.

On the north side of the citadel hill is a terrace (clock-tower) from which there are fine views of the city and surrounding area.

Art Gallery

Bursa's Art Gallery, housed in the Ahmed Vefik Paşa Theatre, displays works by numerous artists, most of them little known outside Turkey. There are a number of works of sculpture which have attracted particular attention.

Location
Cumhuriyet Meydanı

Muradiye Camii (Mosque of Murat II)

Sultan Murat II built the mosque which bears his name in 1447, after Bursa had ceased to be the capital of the Ottoman Empire. A forecourt with cypresses and a beautiful fountain leads into an outer hall with four windows and a doorway, beyond which is an inner hall, its ceiling faced with rare and beautiful tiles.

Location
1·5 km (1 mile) W of city centre

In the gardens of the mosque are ten polygonal domed türbes, their entrances sheltered under overhanging roofs, belonging to Murat II and his family.

Türbes

Of particular interest for their architecture and tiled facings are the Mausoleum of Murat II (with a dome open in the middle so that, in accordance with the Sultan's wish, the rain from heaven should water his grave), the Tomb of Musa, son of Beyazit I (green wall tiles), the Türbe of Şehzade Mustafa (16th c. Persian tiles), the Türbe of Çem, Beyazit II's brother (greenish-blue tiles) and the Türbe of Mahmut.

Türk ve Islâm Eserleri Müzesi (Museum of Turkish and Islamic Art)

The Museum of Turkish and Islamic Art, in the Green Medrese (1414–24), was opened in 1974. It offers an extensive survey of the art of the Ottoman period: candlesticks, pearl and ivory articles, intarsia work, manuscripts, decorated book-covers, screens, sections of beautifully decorated wooden ceilings, weapons, copperware, tiles from İznik and Kütahya, embroidery, ornaments, fine textiles, beautifully worked articles from takkes (dervish convents), calligraphy, gravestones.

Location
Yeşil Medrese
1 km ($\frac{3}{4}$ mile) ESE of city centre

Ulu Camii (Great Mosque)

The Great Mosque was begun in 1379, under Sultan Murat I, and completed by Beyazit and Mehmet I. It is a typical pillared mosque, very much in the Seljuk tradition.

Location
City centre

The entrance, on the north side with its two flanking minarets, leads directly into the main hall, its 20 domes supported on 12 pillars linked by pointed arches. The open central dome and the fountain basin below it give the hall something of the aspect of an inner courtyard. Round the fountain are raised platforms on which worshippers could pray. On the square pillars and the walls are calligraphic inscriptions in the angular Kufic script and the Neshi script. There is a fine cedar-wood mimber of about 1400.

Market scene *Green Mausoleum*

*Uludağ (Mysian or Bithynian Olympus)

Location
17 km (11 miles) S of Bursa

Access
Cableway from Bursa to NW plateau (1700 m (5600 ft)); panoramic road (suitable for buses) to Büyük Uludağ Oteli

Event
Winter Festival of Turkish-American Tourism and Cultural Association

The Uludağ Massif (highest point 2543 m (8344 ft)) is the most popular and best-equipped winter-sports area in Turkey and also, with its forests and Alpine meadows, an excellent holiday area for those seeking rest and relaxation.

The massif consists mainly of granites and gneisses, with some metamorphic rocks higher up, and shows signs of glacial action (corries, etc.). It has preserved very varied vegetation and wildlife.

Uludağ offers numerous viewpoints (many of them reached only by a strenuous walk) from which in good weather the prospect extends to Istanbul and the Bosphorus (see Boğaziçi) or to the Black Sea (see Kara Deniz).

*Yeşil Camii (Green Mosque)

Location
1 km (¾ mile) ESE of city centre

Its sumptuous decoration makes the Green Mosque one of the great master works of Ottoman religious architecture. It was built by Mehmet I between 1419 and 1423 on the site of an earlier Byzantine church. The original minarets, clad with green tiles, were destroyed in the 1855 earthquake, as was the marble vestibule. The doorway with its stalactitic niche, however, is well preserved. There is also a very beautiful marble fountain. The mosque consists of two main halls, one behind the other, and two side rooms on each side, all domed. On either side of the entrance to the central hall are beautiful tiled niches, above which are the Sultan's loge and the women's loges, screened by grilles. In the main hall the base of the walls is covered with the bluish-green tiles from which the mosque takes its name, and above this an inscription runs round the walls. The mihrab is one of the finest of its kind.

*Yeşil Türbe (Green Mausoleum)

Facing the Green Mosque, rather higher up, is the Green Mausoleum of Mehmet I, a domed octagonal building which was originally clad with the green tiles with which parts of the interior walls are still faced. The missing tiles have been replaced by modern reproductions.
On an octagonal base is the Sarcophagus of Mehmet I, with superb tile decoration (flower motifs, calligraphic inscriptions). The beautiful mihrab is in the form of a gateway.
Three of Mehmet's sons are buried beside their father.

Location
1 km (¾ mile) ESE of city centre

Yıldırım Beyazit Camii (Yıldırım Beyazit Mosque)

The Yıldırım Beyazit Mosque was built by Sultan Beyazit I about 1400. It was badly damaged in the 1855 earthquake, and the interior, which is notable for its beautiful marble decoration, was considerably altered in the subsequent restoration. The vestibule has been preserved, however, in its original Early Ottoman form.
The Türbe of Beyazit I and the medrese have recently been restored. There were originally also an imâret and a hamam associated with the mosque.

Location
2 km (1¼ miles) ENE of city centre

*Büyük Çamlıca (Pine-Tree Hill)

Büyük Çamlıca, the highest point in the immediate vicinity of Istanbul (267 m (876 ft)), is one of the most attractive recreation areas within easy reach of the city, both for its variety of vegetation and for the magnificent views to be had from the top, extending in good weather as far as the Black Sea (see Kara Deniz), the Princes' Islands (see Kızıl Adalar) and the Uludağ Massif at Bursa (see entry).
The Television Tower, a steel and concrete needle of the most modern kind, is not at present open to the public.

Location
7 km (4¼ miles) E of city centre on Asiatic side

Bus stop
Ferah Mah

Çanakkale

The largest place on the Dardanelles, situated at the narrowest part of the straits (1244 m (1360 yd)), is Çanakkale (pop. 40,000), chief town of the province of that name, which broadly corresponds to the ancient Troad. It is of considerable importance to tourism as the largest town on this internationally important waterway and the starting-point for a visit to Troy (see entry).
Çanakkale (çanak=pot, kale=castle), named after the pottery industry which flourished here, is a modern town with no historic buildings of any consequence, more particularly because it suffered severe earthquake destruction in 1912. On the west side of the fairly cramped central area of the town is the harbour, with the pier used by the ferry.

Location
250 km (155 miles) WSW of Istanbul as the crow flies

Access
By car or bus from Istanbul via Tekirdağ and Eceabat (ferry to Çanakkale; 345 km (215 miles)), or via Bursa and Bandırma; 545 km (340 miles)); by regular boat direct from Istanbul to Çanakkale

To the north is the newer part of the town, approached by a handsome boulevard. A short distance farther north is the old Castle of Kale Sultaniye (the Sultan's Castle, built by Mehmet II in 1462), opposite which on the European side stands the Castle of Kilidülbahir (End of the Sea). These two Castles of the Straits (Boğaz Hisarları) controlled the Dardanelles at their narrowest point.

Çanakkale Museum contains a variety of material, mainly of the Hellenistic and Roman periods.

Nara

Some 8 km (5 miles) north of Çanakkale is Nara, on the cape of the same name, which probably occupies the site of ancient Nagara. Between Cape Nara and the opposite shore is the second narrowest point (1450 m (1590 yd)) on the Dardanelles, which here turn sharply south. In antiquity, when this was the narrowest point (1300 m (1420 yd)), it was known as the Heptastadion (Seven Stadia) and was crossed by a ferry. It was here that Xerxes, Alexander the Great and the Turks (in 1356) crossed the straits.

Abydos

On a hill to the east was the ancient city of Abydos, which according to Homer belonged to the Trojan Prince Asius. Later colonised by Miletus, its main claim to fame is as the scene of Xerxes' review of his army and the construction of his bridge of boats over the Hellespont during his campaign against Greece in 480 B.C.

Hero and Leander

Abydos and the ancient city of Sestos on the opposite side of the straits are connected with the story of Hero and Leander, as related by the Greek poet Musaeus (end of 6th c. A.D.?) The handsome youth Leander lived in Abydos in Sestos. The two met at a Festival of Aphrodite and fell in love. Then Leander swam across the Hellespont each night to be with his loved one, who lit a beacon on a tower to show him the way. One night, however, the beacon was extinguished in a storm, and Leander was drowned. When his body was washed ashore on the following morning Hero cast herself into the sea so as to be united with her lover in death. Byron repeated Leander's feat in swimming from Abydos to Sestos, as he boasts in "Don Juan".

Troy

See entry

*Çanakkale Boğazı (Dardanelles, Hellespont)

Location
Between the Aegean and the
Sea of Marmara

The Dardanelles, which take their name from the ancient Greek city of Dardanus, are the straits (61 km (38 miles) long, ranging in width between 1·2 km ($\frac{3}{4}$ mile) and 7·5 km ($4\frac{3}{4}$ miles) and in depth between 54 m (177 ft) and 103 m (338 ft)) between the peninsula of Gelibolu (Gallipoli) in Europe and the mainland of Asia Minor which provide a link between the Aegean (and Mediterranean) and the Sea of Marmara and, by way of the Bosphorus, with the Black Sea.

Historical importance of the
Dardanelles

The straits between Europe and Asia have been an important waterway since time immemorial. The excavations at Troy have shown that the Hellespont area (the Sea-coast of Helle, the mythical daughter of Athamas, who fell into the sea here when fleeing from her stepmother) was already settled by man about 3000 B.C. In the 13th c. B.C., the territory was conquered by Achaeans from Greece. The Siege of Troy described in the "Iliad" can be assumed to have taken place at this period. In a second wave of migration the area was occupied by Ionian Greeks. In 480 B.C. Xerxes' Persian army crossed the straits on a bridge of boats, but only a year later, after the Greek naval victory at Mycale, the Hellespont fell to the Athenians. During the Peloponnesian War the Spartans sought to gain control of the straits. In 334 B.C. they were crossed by Alexander the Great.

The Byzantines, for whom free access to the Aegean was vital, fortified both sides of the Hellespont. Thereafter Arab fleets managed on three occasions (in 668, 672 and 717) to force a passage into the Sea of Marmara. On Easter Day 1190, the Emperor Frederick I Barbarossa crossed the Dardanelles with his Crusading army. During the Middle Ages it was the Venetians and Genoese who were principally concerned to maintain freedom of passage through the straits.

In 1356 the Dardanelles fell into the hands of the Ottomans, and Constantinople was thus cut off from the Mediterranean. In 1462 Sultan Mehmet II built two castles at the narrowest point of the straits (1244 m (1360 yd)), Kilidülbahir on the European side and Kale Sultaniye on the Asiatic side at Çanakkale. In 1499, and again in 1657, the Venetians defeated the Turkish fleet at the entrance to the Dardanelles. The Venetians were mainly concerned to secure unrestricted access to the Black Sea, where the Genoese had hitherto enjoyed an almost complete monopoly of trade. Only after the Turkish fleet inflicted a decisive defeat on the Venetians in 1694 did Venice abandon her attacks.

In 1699 Peter the Great demanded free passage for Russian ships. In 1770 the Russian fleet tried, without success, to push into the Dardanelles. Later it defeated the Turkish fleet at Çeşme; and under the Treaty of Küçük Kainarce (1774) Russia secured free passage for its merchant ships. In 1807 a British squadron sailed through the straits to Constantinople; but under a treaty of 1809 between Turkey and Britain, confirmed by the Dardanelles Treaty signed by the five Great Powers in 1841 and by the Peace of Paris in 1856, all non-Turkish warships were prohibited from passing through the straits. During the Crimean War (1853–56) British and French warships made their way into the Black Sea. In 1892 and 1893, under British pressure, the Turkish fortifications on the Dardanelles were considerably strengthened.

At the beginning of the First World War the land fortifications (some of which were somewhat antiquated) comprised three defensive circuits. From February 1915 onwards the Allied fleet tried unsuccessfully to force a passage through the straits; and landings by British, French, Australian, New Zealand and Indian troops on the Gallipoli Peninsula and on the Asiatic coast, from the end of April 1915, were finally beaten off after bitter trench warfare, so that in December the Allies were forced to abandon the Dardanelles adventure after suffering heavy losses. Mustafa Paşa, later President of the Turkish Republic and better known as Atatürk, distinguished himself during the fighting.

After the First World War the Turks secured, together with recognition of their independence, an acknowledgement of their sovereignty over the straits, which had been occupied for a time by the Allies. Under the Treaty of Lausanne (1923) the

Evening in the Dardanelles

Burned Column

Turks were not permitted to fortify the straits, but neither were foreign warships permitted to pass through them. In 1936 Turkey denounced the treaty; and under the Montreux Convention signed in July of that year it was granted the right to refortify the straits and the power, in the event of war, to prohibit the ships of belligerent states from passing through.

At the present time there is an extensive military zone along the Dardanelles, though this does not seriously impede the movement of travellers. Most passenger and cargo ships, however, pass through the Dardanelles at night.

Physical geography of the Dardanelles

The Dardanelles are a former river valley which was drowned as a result of the sinking of the land during the Pleistocene period. The Sea of Marmara came into being at the same time. Clearly visible raised beaches point to a temporary rise in sea-level at certain times in the past. During the warmer weather of the interglacial phases the sea was swollen by water from the melting glaciers and rose above its present level, leaving its mark in the form of abrasions and deposits of gravel. The surplus of water from the Black Sea flows through the Dardanelles and then by way of the Bosphorus and the Sea of Marmara into the Mediterranean. The difference in density between the water of the Black Sea and of the Mediterranean resulting from the inflow of great quantities of fresh water into the Black Sea has the effect of producing a strong surface current flowing at a rate of up to 8·3 km (5·2 miles) an hour from the Sea of Marmara into the Aegean, which makes it difficult for small vessels to enter the Dardanelles, particularly when the so-called "Dardanelles wind" is blowing from the east-north-east, while at the same time heavier water with a high salt content is flowing back along the bottom into the Sea of Marmara at a slower rate.

The hills of Tertiary limestones and marls which rise to heights of 250–375 m (820–1230 ft) along the shores of the Dardanelles have a certain amount of tree cover. The mild and rainy winter climate favours the growing of olives, which constitutes the main source of income for the rural population.

Carpet Museum

See Sultan Ahmet Camii

*Cemberlitaş (Burned Column, Column of Constantine)   D7

The column known locally as Çemberlitaş (Hooped Column) but commonly called the Burned Column or the Column of Constantine was erected in the time of Constantine the Great as the central feature of his Forum. It originally consisted of probably ten porphyry drums, each with a laurel wreath round the top, of which there remain only six. On top of the column was a bronze statue of Constantine, which fell down and was destroyed during a storm about 1105. Originally standing some 50 m (165 ft) high but now reduced to 35 m (115 ft), the column must have suffered damage from weather or fire and was strengthened by hoops round the joins between the drums. The marks left by a fire which ravaged the neighbourhood in the 18th c. can still be seen.

Location
Divan Yolu

Bus stop
Beyazit

Cerrah Paşa Camii (Cerrah Paşa Mosque)   E4

This mosque was built in 1593 by Cerrah Mehmet Paşa, Court Surgeon in the time of Sultan Murat III and Grand Vizier of Mehmet III. The architect was Davut Ağa, a pupil of the celebrated Sinan. The mosque was severely damaged in an earthquake in 1894, but was well and comprehensively restored in 1958–60.

Square in plan, the mosque has a main dome resting on a drum, pierced by 18 windows, which is supported on six "elephants' feet". Still more light is admitted by the windows in the semi-domes surrounding the central dome.

The mimber and mihrab are masterpieces of marble-working, and the galleries with their marble screens are also very beautiful. The vestibule has eight fine marble, granite and porphyry columns.

In the courtyard is the Türbe of Cerrah Paşa and his wife.

Location
Cerrah Paşa Cad.

Bus stop
Aksaray

Chora Monastery

See Kariye Camii

Çiçek Pasajı

See Istiklâl Caddesi

Cihangir Camii (Cihangir Mosque)

Location
Cihangir Caddesi

Bus stop
Kubataş

The Cihangir Mosque, commandingly situated on a hill above the European shore of the Bosphorus, was built by Sultan Süleyman the Magnificent in 1559 as a memorial to his son Cihangir, who died young. The mosque stands on what had been a favourite spot of the dead Prince.

The mosque was originally designed by Sinan but has been much damaged and restored down the centuries. The most recent alterations, in 1889, have made it difficult to discern the original plan.

Çinili Camii (Tiled Mosque)

Location
Çinili Hamam Sok.;
Üsküdar-Toptaşı

Bus stop
Toptaşı

The Tiled Mosque was built by Kasım Aga in 1640 for Kösem Mahpeyker Sultan, wife of Sultan Ahmet I and mother of Sultans Murat IV and Ibrahim.

The charm of this mosque, which externally is relatively plain (square ground-plan, with a single dome and a single minaret) lies in its tile decoration. The conical roof of the mimber, the mihrab, the interior walls and the façade of the vestibule are all faced with Kütahya tiles.

Associated with the mosque are a fountain, a primary school (now a library) and two baths.

Çinili Kösk (Tiled Pavilion)

See Arkeoloji Müzesi

Çırağan Sarayı (Çırağan Palace)   A12

Location
European shore of
Bosphorus

Bus stops
Çırağan, Beşiktaş

Boat landing-stage
Beşiktaş

The Çırağan Palace, situated directly on the shores of the Bosphorus below Yıldız Parkı (see entry), was built by Sultan Abdül Aziz. With its long façade and its lavish architectural display it is in rather similar style to the Dolmabahçe Palace (see entry). Abdül Aziz died in the palace in 1876, in circumstances that are still mysterious, and was succeeded by his nephew Murat V; but after a brief reign Murat was deposed by his brother Abdül Hamit and with his family held prisoner, in the Çırağan Palace. After Murat's death in 1905 the palace stood empty for some time; then in 1908 it became the temporary home of the new Turkish Parliament.

In 1910 the Çırağan Palace was completely destroyed by fire, and since then has remained an unsightly ruin in a setting of great scenic beauty.

The ruins of Çırağan Palace

Constantine Lips Church

See Fenarı İsa Camii

Covered Bazaar

See Kapalı Çarşı

Cumhuriyet Caddesi (Republic Street)   A/B9

Cumhuriyet Caddesi (Republic Street) leads north from Taksim Square (see Taksim Meydanı) and Taksim Park (Taksim Gezi Yeri) to the northern district of Harbiye. This broad avenue is one of Istanbul's most elegant streets, lined with ultra-modern luxury hotels, the showrooms of foreign firms, luxurious shops, banks and airline offices.

Location
Taksim, Harbiye

Bus stops
Taksim, Harbiye

Mete Caddesi, parallel to Cumhuriyet Caddesi on the east, runs from Taksim Square (Opera House) past the University of Technology to the Open-Air Theatre (Açıhava Tiyatrosu).

Mete Caddesi

Dardanelles

See Çanakkale Boğazı

In the gardens of the Maritime Museum

Deniz Müzesi (Maritime Museum)   B11

Location
Dolmabahçe Cad. 119,
Beşiktaş

Bus stop
Beşiktaş

Boat landing-stage
Beşiktaş

Opening times
Wed.–Sun. 9 a.m.–5 p.m.

Admission charge

The Maritime Museum, founded in 1897, has been housed since 1861 in a modern building in the district of Beşiktaş. It illustrates the development of Turkish seafaring and shipping since the establishment of the Ottoman Empire.

Among the most notable exhibits are a map of America by the Turkish Admiral and cartographer Piri Reis (first half of 16th c.); the kayıks (barges) in which the Ottoman Sultans were rowed to their castles on the Bosphorus; Atatürk's cabin from the yacht "Ertugul"; relics of the Crimean War; ship models; wax figures of famous Turkish seamen (including the Greek renegade Hayrettin Barbarossa who helped to build up the Turkish Navy); and portraits of celebrated captains and Ministers of the Navy.

In the gardens are old warships and items of equipment (guns, etc.) of the Turkish Navy.

Dikilitas

See At Meydanı

Divan Museum

See Galata Mevlevihane Müzesi

Dolmabahçe Mosque

Dolmabahçe Camii (Dolmabahçe Mosque)   B10

The Dolmabahçe Mosque was built in 1853 for Bezmi-âlem Sultan, wife of Sultan Mahmut II and mother of Abdül Mecit I. The architect was Serkiz Kalfa Balyan.

The architectural style of the mosque is eclectic, with Baroque features and Renaissance reminiscences. Square in plan, it has four smaller domes round the central dome and is flanked by two tall minarets resembling Corinthian columns.

Large windows admit a flood of light, illuminating the lavish decoration of the interior. Particularly notable are the elaborately wrought red porphyry mihrab and mimber.

Location
Meclisi Mebusan Cad.

Bus stop
Dolmabahçe

Boat landing-stage
Kabataş

*Dolmabahçe Sarayı (Dolmabahçe Palace)   B10/11

The Dolmabahçe Palace was built in 1843–56 (architect Karabet Balyan) for Sultan Abdül Mecit I. This monumental range of buildings, erected on land reclaimed by filling in a small bay on the European shore of the Bosphorus, is still used for State receptions and other great occasions. Atatürk died in the palace in 1938.

The central feature of the palace, which is set in beautiful gardens laid out by a German landscape-gardener named Sester, is the domed Throne Room, on a cruciform plan, which, like the long side wings, shows reminiscences of Renaissance and Classical architecture. The magnificent gateways and imposing marble screen along the edge of the Bosphorus bear

Location
Dolmabahçe Cad.

Bus stop
Dolmabahçe

Boat landing-stage
Kabataş, Beşiktaş

Admission charge

Charge for photography

75

Dolmabahçe Sarayı

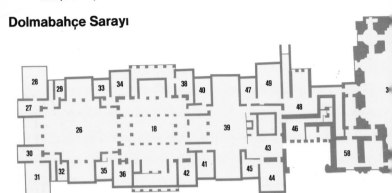

26 Ambassadors' Saloon
27 Interpreters' Room
28 Ambassadors' Waiting-room

30 Antechamber to Red Room
31 Red Room
39 Panoramic Saloon

40 Porphyry Room
43–45 Library
46 Marble Bathroom
47 Music Room

Other rooms are due to be opened to the public shortly

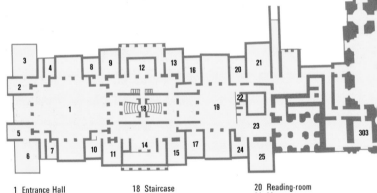

1 Entrance Hall
14 Secretaries' Room

18 Staircase
19 Saloon

20 Reading-room
21 Mosque

witness to former splendours. Adjoining the palace, and standing by itself, is a four-storey Baroque clock-tower.

Entrance Hall

The majestic entrance hall has handsome columns, the bases and fluting of which are coated with gold-leaf. Sèvres and Yıldız vases.

Staircase

In the staircase hall, which has an interesting vaulted roof, hangs a magnificent crystal chandelier. Note also the charming candelabras of crystal and silver and two Indian flower-bowls.

FIRST FLOOR

62 Sultana Mother's
   Reception Room
63 Sultana Mother's
   Bedroom
67 Blue Room
69 Atatürk's Study

71 Room in which
   Atatürk died
73 Sultan Abdül
   Aziz's Bedroom
75 Harem Baths
106 Pink Saloon

110, 111, 114 Bedrooms of Sultan's
   wives
112 Drawing-room of
   Sultan's wives
115 Sultan Resad's Bedroom

GROUND FLOOR

300 Banqueting Hall

84 Sultan Abdül Mecit's Bedroom
Other rooms are due to be opened to the public shortly

In this room foreign ambassadors were received by the Sultan. Notable features are the crystal and silver candelabra and the upholstery and curtains of Hereke silk. The gold-ornamented Sèvres vase on the marble table and the silver clock presented to Sultan Abdül Hamit II on the 25th anniversary of his accession are masterpieces of their kind.

Ambassadors' Saloon

The Red Room was also used for the reception of foreign ambassadors. The mahogany-panelled walls, the red fabrics and the gilded curtain-poles give this room its particular character.

Red Room

Dolmabahçe Sarayı

Dolmabahçe Palace

Porphyry Room	This room has the finest parquet floor in the palace and a remarkable coffered ceiling. The desk, with tortoiseshell and metal inlays, is by Boulle. The Porphyry Room was the scene of many important negotiations and of a meeting between Atatürk and King Edward VIII.
Panoramic Saloon	The Panoramic Saloon was used as a prayer hall and concert hall, and in Atatürk's day as a dining-room. Fine porcelain vases; candelabra; chandelier (60 candles).
Music Room	The special features of this room are the honeycomb-design parquet floor and the painted floor. Fine bergeres upholstered with Hereke silk; grand piano bearing the name Halife Abdülmecit Efendi.
Marble Bathroom	The rest room has a charming sculptured ceiling picked out with gold ornament. The bath itself is of rare Egyptian marble. Adjoining the bathroom is a gallery with numerous portraits of Sultans.
Corridor	A long corridor leads to the Harem. Pictures and vases give it a cheerful air. Beyond the iron door which separated the Harem from the men's apartments is another corridor with paintings by Zonaro, the Court Painter, and Guillemet, the Court Art Teacher.
Apartments of the Sultana Mother	The main rooms in the apartments of the Sultana Mother are the reception-room, with a gold-ornamented marble chimney-piece, an Aubusson carpet and a beautiful domed ceiling, and the bedroom, with a canopied bed and a fine jewelled chest of drawers from Yıldız.

This relatively large room has a fine carved and gilded coffered ceiling. It was used for a variety of ceremonies, including the enthronement of Sultan Abdül Hamit II. Vases; pictures (landscapes); red and white crystal chandelier (54 candles); marble table, with a valuable Baccarat vase.

Blue Room

Adjoining the Blue Room is the room in which Atatürk died. It was used by the last Sultans as a winter room. To the left of the entrance is a beautiful representation of the Four Seasons.

Room in which Atatürk died

This was once the drawing-room of the ladies of the Harem, and was used by Atatürk as a rest-room. Mirrors with gilt carving and chests of drawers similarly ornamented; gold-embroidered upholstery and curtains.

Pink Room

The bedroom of the principal wife has a bed with carved and gilded ornament and walnut veneers on three sides. The second wife's bedroom in red, also has a walnut-veneered bed with bronze ornament. The third wife's bedroom is decorated almost wholly in white. There is also a beautifully painted room in which the Sultan's wives could meet.

Bedrooms of the Sultan's wives

Sultan Resad's bedroom has a canopied bed of walnut and mahogany. Unusual items of furniture are the occasional table and stand by the stove.

Sultan Resad's Bedroom

The Harem Baths consist of a rest-room, dressing-room, wash-room and lavatory, decorated with marble panels and tiles (European designs). The stove in the rest-room is covered with beautiful Kütahya tiles.

Harem Baths

Main gateway

Gardens

Dolmabahçe Sarayı

Staircase

Candelabra

Chimneypiece

Saloon

Notable features of this room are the richly decorated bed, closed in on three sides, a finely carved chair, gilt vases and an Aubusson carpet.

Sultan Abdül Aziz's Bedroom

This room has a canopied bed plated with silver and decorated with mother-of-pearl, two Sèvres vases and a chandelier of coloured crystal.

Sultan Abdül Mecit's Bedroom

The Banqueting Hall is sumptuously decorated. The domed roof is supported on columns, and there is a gallery for the Sultan, with a balcony. Among the most notable of its furnishings are candelabra on marble and porphyry bases and a huge chandelier weighing 4·5 tonnes and carrying 750 candles which was a present to the Sultan from Queen Victoria. The first Turkish Parliament was opened by Abdül Hamit II in the Banqueting Hall on 19 March 1877. In 1927 Atatürk made a speech here which attracted much attention; and here, too, he lay in State before his funeral.

Banqueting Hall

In the Map Saloon, by the stairs to the upper floor, can be seen a large map showing the extent of the Ottoman Empire. The room also contains Baccarat and Yıldız vases.

Map Saloon

The little mosque consists of two adjoining rooms. In front of the mihrab is a Bursa carpet interwoven with gold and silver threads. The mimber is decorated with gold lacquer. Next door to the mosque is the harmoniously designed Reading-room, with a blue-tiled stove and beautiful velvet curtains.

Mosque

The columned Saloon, with windows on both the landward and the seaward sides, has a painted coffered ceiling and very effective *trompe-l'œil* arches on the walls. The carpet in the centre of the room is of Hereke silk.

Saloon

This room has light-coloured tiles, Chinese and cloisonné vases and a Russian porphyry vase.
Between the Saloon and the Secretaries' Room hangs a huge picture, "The Caravan", in a double gilded frame.

Secretaries' Room

---

* Edirne

The provincial capital of Edirne (pop. 70,000) in Turkish Thrace, formerly known as Adrianople, lies at an altitude of 49 m (161 ft) at the junction of the Tunca and the Arda with the Meriç (Maritza), and is an important traffic junction in the Turkish/Greek/Bulgarian frontier area. The second largest town in European Turkey, it is the centre of a fertile agricultural region and in recent years has become a place of rising industrial importance (textiles, leather goods, foodstuffs, perfume).

Location
245 km (152 miles)
NW of Istanbul

Access
By car or bus on the E5N trunk road, or by rail

With its richly furnished mosques, including the magnificent Selimiye Camii, its caravanserais, its low wooden houses and its narrow lanes, Edirne has preserved the character of an old-style Turkish town.

The town was founded about A.D. 125 by the Emperor Hadrian and given the name of Hadrianopolis (Adrianople). Its strategic situation made it a bone of contention between rival Powers. In

History

324 Constantine the Great defeated Licinius here, and in 378 the Emperor Valens was defeated by the Goths near the town. In 586 it was taken by the Avars, in 914 by the Bulgars. It was also harried by the Crusaders, and in 1189–90, during the Third Crusade, the Emperor Frederick Barbarossa established his winter quarters here. In 1205 the Latin Emperor Baldwin was taken prisoner by the Bulgars while marching on Adrianople. In 1362 Edirne was taken by Sultan Murat I and thereafter, until the capture of Constantinople, became the Ottoman capital. In 1829, and again in 1878, it fell briefly into Russian hands; after which its defences were built up as a frontier fortress, which played an important part during the Balkan Wars.

Ali Paşa Çarşısı (Ali Paşa Bazaar)

Location
Saraçılar Cad.

This bazaar, designed by the famous architect Sinan, was built by Hersekli Ali Paşa, one of Sultan Süleyman the Magnificent's

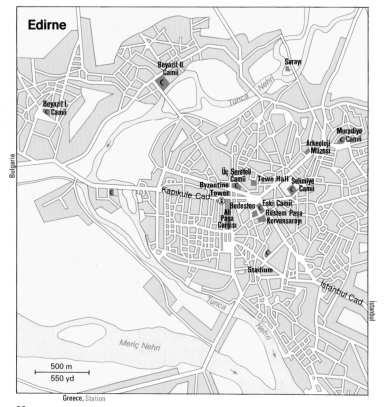

Grand Viziers. Its layout (a covered street of shops with entrances at the ends and on the sides) followed traditional ideas.

Arkeoloji Müzesi (Archaeological Museum)

The Archaeological Museum, originally housed in the primary school of the Selimiye Camii, moved in 1971 into a modern building of its own. It consists of three departments.:

Location
N of Selimiye Camii

Pottery and figures from prehistoric Anatolia; pottery, bronzes and capitals from Thrace (8th c. B.C. onwards); ceramics of the Roman, Byzantine and Islamic periods; glass and copper, silver and gold coins of various periods.

Archaeological Collection

Textiles; rose-water flasks; sewing-boxes; cutlery; writing equipment; weapons (some with fine inlay work); cooking utensils in various materials.

Ethnographic Collection

Anatolian carpets; prayer-mats from Gördes, Bergama and Kirşehir; Thracian and Anatolian kilims, including Şarköy and Turkoman kilims.

Carpets

Bedesten

The Bedesten, now a bazaar for the sale of antiques, was built in the time of Mehmet I. It consists of two vaulted halls roofed with 14 domes, occupied by numerous small shops.

Location
Town centre

Beyazit I Camii (Mosque of Beyazit I)

This mosque in the outer district of Yıldırım was built in the 14th c. in the Bursa style. Its plan is similar to that of a Christian church, with barrel-vaulted side rooms opening off the square vaulted cental hall to form a T-shaped structure. The narthex-like vestibule is linked with the main hall by a narrow passage, on either side of which are domed subsidiary rooms.

Location
W side of town,
beyond the Tunca

*Beyazit II Camii (Mosque of Beyazit II)

The Külliye (mosque complex) of Beyazit II is one of the finest creations of the 15th c. architect Hayrettin. Built between 1484 and 1488, it broadly follows the model of the Sultan Mehmet Fâtih Külliye in Istanbul (see entry).

Location
NW side of town,
beyond the Tunca

The mosque itself is a monumental structure with a single large dome over the prayer hall, the effect of which is enhanced by the two low side rooms, each roofed by nine domes, the low vestibule and the relatively wide forecourt. The interior gains in effect from the abundance of light admitted by the four tiers of windows.

Mosque

Immediately south-west of the mosque is the hospital range, the main elements in which are a domed central structure on an octagonal plan and a medrese of classical type (probably a school of medicine), the two being linked by a courtyard and hall.
To the north-east of the mosque are the imâret (public kitchen), bakery and store-rooms.

Other buildings

Eski Camii (Old Mosque)

Location
Talat Paşa Cad.

The Old Mosque was built in 1414, the architect being Hacı Alattin of Konya. On a square ground-plan, with a nine-domed prayer hall, it follows the pattern of the multi-domed mosque which originated in Bursa (Ulu Camii) (see entry).
The prayer hall is entered from a five-bay vestibule. The mosque is flanked by two minarets erected at different times.

Muradiye Camii (Mosque of Murat II)

Location
NE side of town

This mosque, built by Sultan Murat II about 1429, has a long prayer hall with two domes, flanked by two side halls.
It is entered through a five-bay vestibule built on to the main structure in the manner of a narthex.
Much of the fine interior wall decoration is well preserved. The mihrab is particularly beautiful, with vitrified tiles of outstanding quality.

Rüstem Paşa Kervansarayı (Caravanserai)

Location
SE of town centre

This caravanserai, built by Süleyman the Magnificent's Grand Vizier Rüstem Paşa, was one of a whole series of similar buildings erected along the important east–west highway. Designed by Sinan, it was built about 1560. An imposing rectangular two-storey building, with an inner courtyard and a hamam, it was restored some years ago and is now a hotel.

Sarayı (Palace)

Location
On island in Tunca

There are only scanty remains of this palace and its fortifications, which were almost completely destroyed in 1878.
The palace is believed to occupy the site of a Roman fort built in the time of Hadrian. It is thought that Murat II built a pavilion here in the 15th c.; his son Mehmet II Fâtih added other buildings, and in the 17th c. Mehmet IV enlarged the palace still further. During the 19th c., however, it fell into ruin, and in 1878, after the Russo-Turkish War, it was blown up.

** Selimiye Camii (Mosque of Selim II)

Location
On a hill
E of town centre

The Selimiye Camii, built by Sultan Selim II between 1567 and 1574, is one of the great masterpieces of Ottoman architecture, a mature work produced by the great architect Sinan in his later years. All the elements in the complex – the medrese, the Koranic schools, the covered bazaar, the clock-room – are subordinated to the mosque, flanked by its four minarets, each with three balconies. The mosque itself is on a rectangular ground-plan, with its 45 m (150 ft) high dome (diameter 31·3 m (103 ft)) borne on massive marble and granite columns in octagonal formation, linked by arches. At the corners are small semi-domes.
The interior is sumptuously decorated and furnished. Granite, porphyry and marble columns support the galleries; the

Selimiye Camii, Edirne ▶

stalactitic vaulting, the walls supporting the arches and the skilfully contrived fenestration produce striking light patterns; carefully selected marbles, masterpieces of the tile-maker's art, gilded calligraphic inscriptions and rich ornament create an effect of great splendour, particularly on the mihrab, the mimber and the Sultan's loge; and, contrary to normal practice, the muezzins' tribune is set in the centre of the prayer hall, supported on 12 small columns over a beautiful little ablution fountain.

Museum of Turkish and Islamic Art

In one of the medreses is a Museum of Turkish and Islamic Art, first established in 1925 and reorganised in 1971. In the entrance hall of the museum are inscriptions from Ottoman buildings now destroyed, together with manuscripts of the Koran, tiles, embroidery, glass and weapons. In the Great Hall is a satin tent of the Ottoman period, in which the Viziers conducted their business. In the side rooms are various furnishings and domestic equipment of earlier days, medals, calligraphic inscriptions and drinking-cups. In the garden are tombs of various dates since the 15th c., including that of Siddi Şah Sultan, wife of Mehmet the Conqueror.

*Uç Şerefeli Camii (Three-Balconied Mosque)

Location
Cumhuriyet Meydanı

The name of this mosque comes from the three balconies (üç = three, şerefe = balcony) on the minaret on the south side. Built by Sultan Murat II (15th c.), it shows the transition between the Bursa style and the Classical style. An earthquake in 1752 caused severe damage to the mosque, which was subsequently repaired with much painstaking effort.

The mosque is rectangular in plan, but is roofed by a hexagonal vaulted central dome and by four large and three small lateral domes. An innovation in mosque architecture seen here for the first time is the inner court surrounded by dome-roofed arcades.

The four minarets at the corners of the courtyard differ in form. The one at the south corner is the most massive, with the three balconies which give the mosque its name; the baklavalı minare (rhomboid minaret) has two balconies, the çubuklu minare (striped minaret) and the burmalı minare (spiral minaret) each have one.

Edirnekapısı Camii

See Mihrimah Camii

Egyptian Bazaar

See Mısır Çarsısı

Egyptian Obelisk

See At Meydanı, Dikilitaş

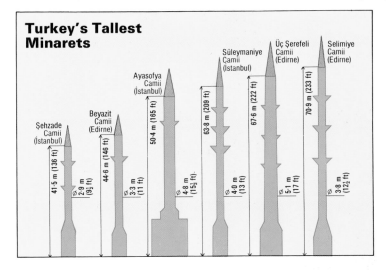

Turkey's Tallest Minarets

Şehzade Camii (İstanbul): 41·5 m (136 ft), ∅ 2·9 m (9½ ft)

Beyazit Camii (Edirne): 44·6 m (146 ft), ∅ 3·3 m (11 ft)

Ayasofya Camii (İstanbul): 50·4 m (165 ft), ∅ 4·8 m (15½ ft)

Süleymaniye Camii (İstanbul): 63·8 m (209 ft), ∅ 4·0 m (13 ft)

Üç Şerefeli Camii (Edirne): 67·6 m (222 ft), ∅ 5·1 m (17 ft)

Selimiye Camii (Edirne): 70·9 m (233 ft), ∅ 3·8 m (12½ ft)

Eminönü   D7

The Eminönü district is the "pulsating heart" of İstanbul, the junction of all the city's main transport systems (landing-stage of the Bosphorus and Princes' Islands boats and the ferry services to Üsküdar, Çanakkale and İzmir; terminus of the Orient line of the European railway network; one of the city's busiest bus stations; south end of Galata Bridge (see entry). Within this area is a great concentration of large commercial houses, banks and insurance companies, industrial firms, public offices and other large service organisations; and here, too, are the Egyptian Bazaar (Mısır Çarşısı) and the outlying parts of the Great Bazaar (Kapalı Çarşısı – see entries), their busy and colourful activity extending northward to the New Mosque (Yeni Camii – see entry).

Location
At mouth of Golden Horn (south side)

Bus stop
Eminönü

Boat landing-stage
Eminönü

Suburban railway station
Sirkeci

*Emirgân

The picturesque village of Emirgân, on the European shore of the Bosphorus, perpetuates the name of a Persian nobleman, a friend of Sultan Murat IV, who had a country house here.
In the friendly little village square is a mosque built by Sultan Abdül Hamit I, in the Baroque style of the seond half of the 18th c. Also of interest from the architectural point of view is the yalı (mansion) of Şerif Abdullah Paşa of Mecca, which is now a museum.

Location
16 km (10 miles) N of city centre on European side of Bosphorus

Bus stop
Emirgân

Boat landing-stage
Emirgan

Emirgân

Tulip Gardens

Opening times
Daily 8.30 a.m.–5.30 p.m.

Admission charge

Above the village are the world-famous Tulip Gardens of Emirgân, which attract tens of thousands of visitors every spring. There are over a thousand different varieties of tulip, including the legendary black tulip. Every year at the end of April and beginning of May the celebrated Tulip Festival (see Practical Information – Events) is held here.

Eski Bedesten

See Kapalı Çarsı

Eski Saray

See Topkapı Sarayı

Eski Şark Eserleri Müzesi

See Arkeoloji Müzesi

---

*Eyüp   A3

Location
Head of Golden Horn,
west side

Bus stop
Eyüp

Boat landing-stage
Eyüp

The Istanbul suburb of Eyüp, lying on the west side of the Golden Horn in attractive hilly country, has long been a favourite resort of the people of Istanbul, and in spite of modern housing and factory development it has managed to retain its romantic rural charm. The Eyüp Camii, the most sacred of Istanbul's mosques, the extensive Turkish cemeteries, the beautiful cypress groves and the picturesque views it offers make Eyüp well worth a visit.

*Eyüp Camii (Eyüp Mosque)   A3

The Eyüp Camii is the most sacred of Istanbul's mosques and the holiest shrine of Islam after the holy places in Mecca, Medina and Jerusalem. It bears the name of Eyüp Ensarî, a friend of the Prophet Muhammad and standard-bearer of the first armies of the faith, who was killed during the First Arab Siege of Constantinople (674–678) and is said to have been buried here.

Building history

In1458 Sultan Mehmet the Conqueror built a mausoleum and a mosque in honour of Eyüp Ensarî. In the early 18th c. Sultan Ahmet III enlarged the mosque and erected two tall minarets. Towards the end of the century Sultan Selim III undertook a major rebuilding of the mosque, which had fallen into disrepair, and it was reopened for worship in 1800.

Cemetery, Eyüp

View over the Golden Horn from Piyer Loti

Eyüp

Mosque

The mosque, built on a rectangular plan, is similar in structure to the Azapkapı Camii (see entry). The main dome is borne on eight columns and is surrounded by four large and four small semi-domes. Notable features of the interior are the beautiful marble mihrab and mimber, enriched with gold ornament, and the ceiling-painting.

Courtyard

The mosque courtyard, shaded by plane trees, has Baroque gateways and is surrounded on three sides by elegant dome-roofed halls in which the Sultan on his accession was girded with the sword of Osman.

Türbe of Eyüp

Facing the entrance to the mosque is the Türbe of Eyüp, sheltered by a plane tree enclosed within a railing. This domed tomb is faced externally and internally with supremely beautiful tiles of the 16th–19th c. Other beauties of the interior are the silver candlesticks and screen, and the "wishing window" inserted by Sultan Ahmet I.

Other buildings

Other buildings belonging to the mosque complex are a public kitchen, a Koranic school, a fountain and a number of tombs in the adjoining cemeteries, including the türbes of Mihrişah Valide Sultan (1795), Hüsrev Paşa (1825), Pertev Paşa (1772), Sultan Mehmet V (1922), Ferhat Paşa (1504), Sokullu Mehmet Paşa (1579) and Siyavus Paşa (1611).

Cemeteries

Above the Eyüp Camii, to the north, are extensive cemeteries, which are well worth a visit, not only for the sake of the interesting tombstones carved with symbolic devices (a turban signifying a man, a broken rose, a young girl, etc.), but also for the beautiful views. In Christian times there was a church here dedicated to SS. Cosmas and Damian.

*Piyer Loti

The popular Teahouse of Pierre Loti (Piyer Loti), on the edge of the cemetery, was a favourite haunt of the French writer. From here there is a beautiful view over the Golden Horn down to Stamboul and Pera.

Zal Mahmut Paşa Camii (Zal Mahmut Paşa Mosque)

Location
Defterdar Cad.

This mosque was built by Sinan, probably after 1551, for Zal Mahmut Paşa, son-in-law of Süleyman the Magnificent. The architect contrived to link the mosque architecturally with two medreses and the türbe of the founder and his wife. The façade is strikingly effective with its alternate courses of dark brick and light-coloured stone.

The mosque, cubic in shape with a relatively shallow dome and small octagonal turrets, has an unusually high side wall (necessitated by the fall in the ground), which extends down to the lower courtyard.

The interior also shows interesting architectural features. The dome is set low on the cube like a canopy, and the arches on which it rests start at the level of the galleries. The normal walls supporting the arches are missing on three sides.

The türbe of the founder and his wife is also unusual. The exterior is octagonal but the interior is on a cruciform plan. Effective features of the interior are the variations in the placing of the windows and the projecting corners.

Fâtih Camii (Fâtih Mosque)

See Sultan Mehmet Fâtih Külliyesi

Fenarı İsa Camii (Fenarı İsa Mosque; Church of Constantine Lips)   D4

The Fenarı İsa Mosque arose in the 15th c. by the reconstruction of two adjacent Byzantine churches. It was extensively damaged by fire in 1917. The more northerly of the two churches was built in the 10th c. by a high Imperial dignitary named Constantine Lips, and was dedicated to the Theotokos (Mother of God); the other church, dedicated to St John the Baptist, was built by the Empress Theodora at the end of the 13th c.

For some years scholars from the Byzantine Institute of America have been attempting to unravel the architectural history of the ruins. Some parts have already been restored.

Location
Vatan Cad./Halıcılar Cad.

Bus stop
Vatan Cad.

Fethiye Camii

* Fethiye Camii (Mosque of the Conquest; Pammakaristos Monastery)   C4

Location Fethiye Cad. **Bus stop** Fener	The origins of the Pammakaristos Monastery go back to the 11th c. After the Turkish Conquest of Constantinople it continued for more than 130 years to be the seat of the Orthodox Patriarchate, and it was only in 1591 that Sultan Murat III made the monastery over to Islam in celebration of his victories over Georgia and Azerbaijan. The building was thoroughly restored in the reign of Sultan Abdül Mecit. During the present century mosaics and frescoes were discovered in the church, and after painstaking restoration these are now once again visible.
Architecture	The plan of the church is not easy to follow, since it was built in a number of stages. The church proper and the narthex date from the time of the Comneni. The parekklesion on the south side of the church was added in the 14th c. for Michael Glabas and his family. The ambulatory on the north side and the external narthex at the west end are Late Byzantine. During the conversion of the church into a mosque, the Islamic architects were concerned to increase the space in the interior, which seriously distorted the original structure.
Parekklesion	The parekklesion has been restored in exemplary fashion. The mosaic in the dome depicts Christ Pantocrator, surrounded by Prophets. In the apse are Christ Hyperagathos, the Mother of God, John the Baptist and the Four Archangels. On the soffits of the arches and elsewhere are saints and hierarchs. In the south aisle is the Baptism of Christ.

Firuz Ağa Camii (Firuz Ağa Mosque)   E7

Location Divan Yolu **Bus stop** Sultanahmet	This graceful little mosque, a square-domed structure, was founded in 1491 by Firuz Ağa, Treasurer to Sultan Beyazit II. It has beautiful stalactitic ornament not only under the main dome but also on the capitals in the vestibule with its three small domes. Beside the mosque is the dignified tomb of its founder.
Hippodrome	See At Meydanı

Fish Market

See İstiklâl Caddesi, Balık Pazarı

** Galata Köprüsü (Galata Bridge)   C/D7

Location Eminönü-Karaköy **Bus stops** Eminönü, Karaköy	The Galata Bridge, long a byword for chaotic traffic conditions and still a very busy traffic artery in spite of the relief brought by the new motorway bridge (see Haliç), spans the mouth of the Golden Horn at its junction with the Bosphorus. The first Galata Bridge, a timber structure, was built in 1845.

View of the Bosphorus from the Galata Tower

Galata Bridge and Tower

A wooden house in the old town

Boat landing-stages
Eminönü, Karaköy, Galata
Köprüsü

This was replaced by a new bridge in 1863, followed by another in 1877. The present bridge was constructed by a German firm in 1909–12.

The bridge is 468 m (512 yd) long and 26 m (85 ft) wide. It rests on 22 pontoons. The middle section swivels to allow ships to pass into and out of the Golden Horn.

The lower (pontoon) level of the bridge is used as landing-stages for local boat traffic and also provides accommodation for fishmongers and other traders.

*Galata Kulesi (Galata Tower)   C7

Location
Galipdede Cad.

Bus stop
Tünel

Funicular station
Tünel

Opening times
10 a.m. to midnight

The Galata Tower occupies a site where there is believed to have been a tower as early as the 5th–6th c. In 1338 the Genoese built a massive watch-tower here to protect their largely independent settlement of Pera (Galata), and in 1446 this was strengthened and heightened. In Ottoman times it was used as a fire-watching post and prison. It suffered a variety of damage in the course of its history, including destruction by fire in 1794 and again in 1843. In 1875 the upper part of the tower was rebuilt, and just under 100 years later its original conical roof was restored.

The viewing-platform of the tower, which stands 68 m (223 ft) high, is 140 m (460 ft) above sea-level, and affords superb views of the city, the Golden Horn and the south end of the Bosphorus. Since its recent renovation the tower has become a popular tourist attraction, offering not only a beautiful view but a Turkish coffee-house, a Genoese tavern, a luxury restaurant and an excellent night-club, with Oriental floor shows and belly-dancing.

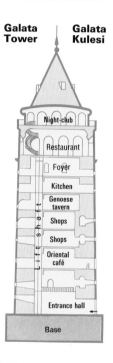

Galata Tower   Galata Kulesi

Night-club
Restaurant
Foyer
Kitchen
Genoese tavern
Shops
Shops
Oriental café
Entrance hall
Base

*Galata Mevlevihane Müzesi (Dervish Convent; Divan Museum)   C7

Location
Galipdede Cad.

Funicular stations
Tünel, İstiklâl Cad.

Bus stop
Tünel

The Galata Mevlevihane, the first dervish convent in Istanbul, was founded by İskender Paşa in 1491. It was burned down in 1765 but rebuilt soon afterwards. The convent, frequently described by visitors to Istanbul, particularly in the 19th c., was closed after the proclamation of the Republic. Restoration of the building was begun in 1965, and it now houses the Divan Museum, which gives an interesting picture of life in a dervish convent. Associated with it are a Literary Museum and a well-stocked library, with a display of works by the famous lyric poet and mystic Şeyh Galip.

In the cemetery of the convent are the graves of prominent members of the Mevlana Order, including Ismail Rusuhi Dede, Şeyh Galip, Esrar Dede, Fesih Dede and Gavsi Dede.

Cemetery

Golden Horn

See Haliç

Great Bazaar

See Kapalı Çarşı

Greek Orthodox Patriarchate

See Haghios Georgios

Gül Camii (Rose Mosque; Church of St Theodosia)　　　　　　　C5

The Byzantine Church of St Theodosia, probably built in the 11th c., was converted into a mosque in the reign of Sultan Selim II. The name of Rose Mosque refers to various legends connected with its building.

The architecture of the mosque follows the pattern of the Byzantine domed cruciform church with its characteristic galleries in the transepts. The original church, however, was considerably altered after its conversion into a mosque; in particular the central dome and its supporting structures were rebuilt.

Location
Mektep Sok.

Bus stop
Unkapan

Gülhane Parkı (Rose-Garden Park)　　　　　　　　　　　　D8/9

Gülhane Parkı, which surrounds Topkapı Sarayı (see entry) and extends to the tip of the promontory, is now a public park, with a small zoo and other attractions.

In the park rises the Goth's Column, one of Istanbul's lesser-known antiquities. This 15 m (50 ft) high granite monolith with a Corinthian capital bears an inscription, "Fortunae reduci ob devictos Gothos", commemorating a Byzantine victory over the Goths. The column is said to have been topped by a statue of Byzas, the original founder of the city.

On the tip of Seraglio Point, beyond the coast road, is a statue of Atatürk by the Austrian sculptor Kripple (1926).

A little way west stands a 17th c. pavilion, Sepetçiler Köskü, restored some years ago.

Location
Seraglio Point

Bus stop
Gülhane Park

95

Evening on the Golden Horn

Haghia Eirene

See Aya İrini Kilisesi

Haghia Sophia

See Ayasofya

Haghios Georgios   C4
(St George's Church; Greek Orthodox Patriarchate, Ortodoks Patrikhanesi)

Location
Near Sadrazam Ali Paşa Cad.

Bus stop
Fener

This plain and modest little church, built in 1720, follows the plan of the Early Christian basilicas.

In the nave is the magnificent throne of the Greek Orthodox Patriarch, probably dating from the Late Byzantine period. In the south aisle are the sarcophagi of SS. Euphemia of Chalcedon, Omonia and Theophano, whose remains are the church's principal treasures.

Facing the church are the offices of the Patriarchate, completed only after 1941. Within the precincts of the Patriarchate Gregory V, Patriarch of Constantinople, was hanged for treason in 1821, at the beginning of the Greek War of Independence.

*Halic (Golden Horn)

A–D3–7

The Golden Horn, the 11 km (7 mile) long inlet (up to 40 m (130 ft) deep) which opens off the Bosphorus between Stamboul and Pera, is rated the best natural harbour in the world. It is particularly photogenic on fine evenings. Geologists interpret it as a drowned river valley, the result of the tectonic sinking of the Aegean coastal region in the Early Pleistocene Age and the falls in sea-level during the Ice Age.

Boat trips
From Galata Bridge

Haliç Köprüsü (Golden Horn Bridge)

A/B3/4

This 960 m (1050 yd) long motorway bridge over the Golden Horn, also known as Fâtih Köprüsü (Conqueror Bridge), was opened for traffic in 1973. It is part of the fine new ring road which bypasses the city on the north and continues over the Bosphorus Bridge (see Boğaziçi Köprüsü) into Asia Minor.

Location
Ayvansaray-Halicioğlu

Harem

See Topkapı Sarayı

Haseki Camii (Haseki Mosque)

D/E3

The Haseki Mosque was built in 1530 by Hürrem Sultan, wife of Süleyman the Magnificent. It was long attributed to Sinan, but there is now some doubt whether it was designed by him. Originally the mosque had only a single dome. The second was added in the time of Sultan Ahmet I.
To the north, on the opposite side of the street, are the medrese, primary school, hospital and public kitchen, all part of the mosque complex.
Some of the finest tiles from the medrese can now be seen in the Tiled Pavilion (see Arkeologi Müzesi).

Location
Haseki Cad., Aksaray

Bus stop
Aksaray

*Haseki Hürrem Hamamı (Baths of Roxelana)

E8

These double baths, built by Sinan for the wife of Süleyman the Magnificent, are one of the most unusual buildings of the kind. At the two ends of the structure are the main bath halls, which are square domed rooms; next to these are the two rest-rooms, each with three small domes, and beyond these are the two octagonal sweating-rooms, each with four niches in the sides and four small cabins in the corners.
The baths are at present being restored for use as a museum.

Location
At Meydanı

Bus stop
Sultanahmet

Haydarpaşa

D–F11/12

Haydarpaşa, an old port on the Asiatic side of the Bosphorus, was the starting-point of the Baghdad Railway which was built at the beginning of this century with German assistance. In

Location
S end of Bosphorus (Asiatic side)

Haydarpaşa

New port installations at Haydarpaşa and Harem

Boat landing-stage
Haydarpaşa

recent years, with the extension and modernisation of the port installations, it has enjoyed increasing prosperity.

Selimiye Camii (Mosque of Selim III) D/E12

Location
Near Selimiye Kışlası, Harem

Bus stop
Harem

Boat landing-stage
Harem

The Selimiye Mosque was built by Sultan Selim III in 1804. It was renovated in the 1950s.

This single-domed mosque, with two minarets, shows a number of unusual architectural features: note, for example, the lanterns over the corner pillars and the volutes topping the pillars.

The woodwork, stonework and embroidery in the interior are of excellent quality. The entrance doorway has a very fine bronze door-knocker.

Selimiye Kışlası (Selimiye Barracks) E11/12

Location
Above Harem İskelesi

Bus stop
Harem

Boat landing-stage
Harem İskelesi

This gigantic building, not unlike the Escorial near Madrid, occupies a prominent situation on the Asiatic side of the Bosphorus at its southern end. It consists of four wings, three storeys high, set round a large parade-ground, with towers at the four corners. Construction of the barracks began in 1826, in the reign of Sultan Mahmut II, but the building took a quarter of a century to complete. The architect was Kirkor Balyan. During the Crimean War the barracks became a British military hospital, and it was here that Florence Nightingale did so much to improve the medical and nursing services of the British forces. There is a small museum in her honour in the north-east tower of the barracks.

Hekimoğlu Ali Paşa Camii (Hekimoğlu Ali Paşa Mosque)   E3

This mosque was built in 1734 by Hekimoğlu Ali Paşa, Grand Vizier in the reigns of Mahmut I and Osman III. The architect is believed to have been Ömer Ağa.
The main dome of the mosque, which is square in plan, is supported by semi-domes, with massive columns supporting the carefully contrived vaulting. A notable feature of the interior is the mihrab, which projects from the main structure like the choir of a Christian church.
The tiles in the interior are Istanbul-made of the 18th c. There is a graceful marble mimber.

Over the arched gateway in the courtyard of the mosque is a small library with an attractive loggia. Also in the courtyard is the türbe of the founder, with an ablution fountain. At the entrance to the courtyard can be seen a drinking-fountain with a beautifully worked bronze grille.

Location
Hekimoğlu Ali Paşa Cad., Koçamustafapaşa

Bus stop
Koçamustafapaşa

Courtyard

Hellespont

See Çanakkale Boğazı

Hippodrome

See At Meydanı

Hırka-ı Şerif Camii (Hırka-ı Şerif Mosque)   C3

This pilgrim shrine, the Mosque of the Holy Mantle, was founded by Sultan Abdül Mecit in 1850. In Empire style, with two minarets, it stands on a high terrace and departs somewhat from the norm with its octagonal ground-plan and relatively low dome.
In a special domed chamber in front of the mihrab is preserved one of Istanbul's principal relics, a mantle of the Prophet. The pious Muslim visits the precious relic on or after the 15th day of Ramadan.
The mihrab, mimber and Kuran kürsü, elaborately carved, are of beautifully coloured and highly polished porphyry. Some of the calligraphic inscriptions are in the hand of Sultan Abdül Mecit himself, others are by the renowned calligrapher Mustafa İzzet Efendi.

Location
Between Fâtih Mosque and Edirne Gate

Bus stop
Atikali

Imperial Palace

See Tekfur Sarayı

İmrahor Camii (İmrahor Mosque; Monastery of Studius)   F2

Location
Near İmrahor İlias Bey Cad.

Bus stop
Yedikule

Suburban railway station
Yedikule

The Monastery of Studius, now a ruin, is one of Istanbul's oldest Christian buildings, going back to a 5th c. foundation. In the course of its history the monastery – in which the relics of John the Baptist (now displayed in Topkapı Sarayı) were probably preserved – became one of the great spiritual centres of the Byzantine Empire. It played a leading role in the Iconoclastic conflict of the 8th and 9th c.; during the 10th, 11th and 12th c. it supplied Constantinople with several patriarchs; and the Emperors Isaac I and Michael VII Ducas were educated in the monastery.

The monastic church was converted into a mosque by Beyazit II's Master of the Horse. It was severely damaged by a fire in the 18th c. and an earthquake in 1894.

The church is basilican in form, with an apse at the east end and two rows of verd antique columns dividing it into three aisles. There is a fine *opus sectile* pavement with remains of figural representations. The columned narthex was originally two-storeyed and must have been one of the most beautiful of the kind.

Independence Monument

See Taksim Meydanı

*İstiklal Caddesi   B/C7/8
(Independence Street; formerly Grande Rue de Péra)

Bus stops
Tünel, Galatasaray, Taksim

Funicular station
Tünel

İstiklal Caddesi (Independence Street), the ever-busy main axis of the Western-style new district of Beyoğlu (formerly Pera), runs north from Tünel Meydanı (at the top of the Tünel funicular (see entry)) to Galatasaray Meydanı and then bears north-east to Taksim Meydanı (Taksim Square). All along this street a series of imposing buildings bear witness to the splendours of earlier days when the Grande Rue de Péra was lined with foreign embassies, exclusive shops and expensive restaurants. After a fairly long period when there was little new development, modern buildings such as the Odakule in the lower half of the street are pointing the way towards the pattern of the future.

Churches and fine houses

Near Tünel Meydanı are the Swedish Consulate (No. 497; a 17th c. building), the Consulate-General of the Soviet Union (No. 443; built 1843 by the Fossati brothers), the Church of St Mary Draperis (No. 431), founded by Franciscans in the 16th c. and altered in the 18th c., and the Netherlands Consulate (No. 393; 17th c.). Off to the right, in Tomtom Sokağı, the Italian Consulate occupies a 19th c. Venetian palazzo. Farther north, in Nuriziya Sokağı, is the 19th c. Palais de France, formerly the residence of the French Ambassador. Close by stands the Church of St Louis (R.C.) Just before Galatasaray Meydanı, on the right, is the early 20th c. Church of St Anthony; on left the Greek Orthodox Church of the Panaghia (19th c.). On the corner of Galatasaray Meydanı, on the left, is the Beyoğlu Post Office and off on the left, a short

İstiklâl Caddesi

Odakule

distance away in Meşrutiyet Caddesi, the United Kingdom Consulate. On the east side of the square, set in gardens, is the select Galatasaray Lisesi, which at the time of its foundation in the 19th c. was one of Istanbul's most important schools. From Galatasaray Meydanı İstiklâl Caddesi continues north-east past the little Ağa Camii (Ağa Mosque) on the left to the Greek Orthodox Church of the Trinity (consecrated 1882; Byzantine icons) and the French Consulate. It then runs into Taksim Square.

At the Post Office the inconspicuous little Çiçek Pasajı branches off İstiklâl Caddesi. This flower and fish market is one of the most interesting corners of Istanbul, to which its bustling life, alcohol-laden atmosphere, aroma of exotic spices and interesting local characters attract crowds of visitors throughout the day and late into the night. At the end of Çiçek Pasajı is the Fish Market (Balık Pazarı) proper, in which a bewildering range of fish and seafood is offered for sale. In a little lane which runs north from the Fish Market, Kirizantem Pasajı (Chrysanthemum Passage), are some of Istanbul's most characteristic taverns and tea-houses.

Çiçek Pasajı

In recent years a lively entertainments quarter, of the type found in large Western cities, has grown up on both sides of the upper part of İstiklâl Caddesi. Here tourists and devotees of night life, mostly from the large hotels in Taksim Square, come to enjoy the wide variety of entertainments offered – in cinemas showing low-class sex films, in old taverns and tea-houses which have recently been metamorphosed into casinos and bars with or without floor shows, but also in old-established

Entertainments district

places of entertainment where, as an alternative to striptease, visitors can occasionally see belly-dancing shows.

*İznik (Nicaea)

Location 185 km (115 miles) (by road) SE of Istanbul	The town of İznik (Nicaea) lies on the intensively cultivated eastern shore of İznik Gölü, a large lake (area 303 sq. km (117 sq. miles), maximum depth 80 m (245 ft), altitude 80 m (260 ft) in the valley which extends from Gemlik Bay into the western Pontic Mountains.
History	İznik occupies the site of ancient Nicaea, founded in the 4th c. B.C. by Antigonus, one of Alexander the Great's generals. The town, originally called Antigoneia, was renamed about 305 B.C. by King Lysimachus of Thrace in honour of his wife Nicaea. In 281 B.C. it fell to the Bithynians. The town was damaged by earthquakes on a number of occasions, but after its rebuilding by the Emperor Hadrian enjoyed a period of great prosperity. In Christian times it became the see of a bishop, and although burned down by the Goths in 259 retained its importance. In 325 the First Ecumenical Council was held here. In 364 Valentinian was proclaimed Emperor in Nicaea. During the reign of Justinian the town grew still further. In 787 it was again prominent as the scene of the Seventh Ecumenical Council, which re-established the veneration of images and condemned the Iconoclasts. In 1074 the town was captured by the Seljuks, but 23 years later was retaken by the Crusaders. From 1204 to 1261, when Constantinople was held by the Latin Emperors, Nicaea was the seat of the Eastern Roman Emperor. The town was taken by the Ottomans in 1331. In 1514 Sultan Selim I brought in numbers of potters from Tabriz and Azerbaijan, establishing the tile industry from which İznik became renowned.

Fortifications

	The principal sight of İznik is its circuit of walls, reminiscent of the walls of Constantinople. Although partly ruined and overgrown with vegetation, they are still immensely impressive. Of the old Greek fortifications little is left. In the 1st c. A.D. the Romans altered the line of the walls, originally on a square plan, to form a polygon with a total perimeter of 4427 m (4842 yd). In Byzantine times the gateways were heightened and flanked by towers. The finest stretch of walls, reusing earlier masonry, dates from the reign of Leo the Isaurian (8th c.; inscription). A considerable length of wall is of Seljuk construction. The inner circuit of walls is 9 m (30 ft) high and 3·5 m (11½ ft) thick, and originally had a battlemented wall-walk. It incorporates 108 towers, which are accessible from the town side. Outside these walls is an outer ward up to 16 m (52 ft) deep, and beyond this a lower wall with round towers and a moat.
Lefke Gate	At the most easterly point in the walls stands the fourfold Lefke Gate, like a Roman triumphal arch, which was built about A.D. 70. Outside the gate is the end of an aqueduct, probably constructed in the time of Justinian and renovated by Sultan Orhan.

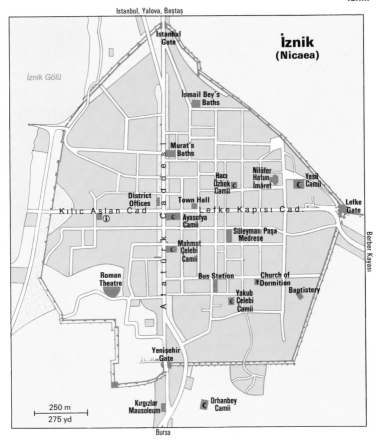

The Istanbul Gate, at the most northerly point in the circuit, is similar to the Lefke Gate. On an inner wall dating from a later period are two interesting masks.

Istanbul Gate

The oldest part of the Yenişehir Gate, on the south side of the town, dates from the 3rd c. A.D. (inscription in the name of the Emperor Claudius Gothicus).

Yenişehir Gate

Yeşil Camii (Green Mosque)

A short distance north-west of the Lefke Gate we come to the Yeşil Camii (Green Mosque), İznik's most beautiful mosque. It was built in 1384–89 by Hayrettin Paşa Grand Vizier to Sultan Murat I. The vestibule has three arcades borne on two granite columns. Only fragments of the original marble screens survive. There are sumptuous doorway and windows flanked by calligraphic inscriptions.

Location
Near Lefke Gate

103

The ancient walls of İznik

Nilûfer Hatun İmâreti (Public Kitchen)

Location
Near Yeşil Camii

To the west of the Green Mosque is a public kitchen, built in 1388 by Nilûfer Hatun. Sultan Orhan's wife. It now houses the Municipal Museum (Greek and Roman antiquities, gravestones, İznik tiles, inscriptions).

Ayasofya Camii (Haghia Sophia)

Location
Town centre

The ruins of Haghia Sophia are in the centre of the town, at the intersection of the two main streets which lead to the four ancient gates. This was probably the meeting-place of the Seventh Ecumenical Council (787). A three-aisled basilica with small domed rooms on either side of the apse, the present church was built in 1065, replacing an earlier church of the time of Justinian. In the reign of Sultan Orhan it was converted into a mosque and enriched with beautiful tiled decoration.

Church of the Dormition (Koimesis)

Location
SE of old town

The Church of the Dormition, once a large domed basilica, was built in the 11th c. Near by, to the east, is the 6th c. Baptistery.

Roman Theatre

Location
SW of old town

In the south-western quarter of the old town is the Roman Theatre, believed to have been built in A.D. 112 by the Roman

Governor, Pliny the Younger. Since there was no natural hill into which the theatre could be built, the seating is borne on masssive and beautifully constructed vaulting, set at an angle to bear the weight.

Berber Kayası (Barber's Rock)

1 km (¾ mile) east of the Lefke Gate is the Barber's Rock, with the remains of a 4 m (13 ft) long sarcophaguş. From the top of the hill there is a superb view of the town of İznik and its lake.

Location
1 km (¾ mile)
E of Lefke Gate

Beştaş (Obelisk of Cassius)

5 km (3 miles) north-west of İznik, on the edge of the hills, stands the Obelisk of Cassius, the 12 m (39 ft) high tomb of C. Cassius Philiscus (2nd c. A.D.).

Location
5 km (3 miles) NW of İznik

Kadıköy   F12

Kadıköy (Judge's Village), a fashionable residential area, lies on the Asiatic shore at the northern end of the Sea of Marmara. This was the site of the Greek colony of Chalcedon which controlled the Asiatic side of the Bosphorus, and in Roman times became capital of the province of Bithynia. The Fourth Ecumenical Council was held here in 451.

Location
Asiatic side of
Sea of Marmara

Bus stop Kadıköy

Boat landing-stage
Kadıköy

Kadıköy: the landing-stage

* **Kalenderhane Camii** (Kalenderhane Mosque; Kyriotissa Church) D6

Location
Mart Şehitleri Cad.

Bus stop
Beyazit Meydanı

The Kalenderhane Mosque, originally a Byzantine church, has been the subject of intensive study and investigation in recent years, and is now in course of restoration.

The former Church of the Mother of God Kyriotissa stands on a site near the Aqueduct of Valens which was originally occupied by public baths built about A.D. 500. In the 6th c., part of the bathing establishment was pulled down and replaced by a small church, to which two side chapels were added some time later. In the 12th c. this gave place to the present domed cruciform church. From 1204 to 1261, during the Latin Empire, it became a Roman Catholic church and was decorated with a cycle of frescoes of scenes from the life of St Francis of Assisi. Thereafter it reverted to the Orthodox faith, and in the 15th c. was converted into a mosque for wandering dervishes (Kalenderiye).

Architecture

The Kalenderhane Camii is a typical domed cruciform church with an inner and an outer narthex. The northern and southern arms of the cross are closed by walls with three tiers of windows and triple arcades. The exterior is striking, with alternating courses of red bricks and white stone.

Paintings and mosaics

The most recent investigations in the interior of the church have yielded sensational results in the form of paintings and mosaics of the Byzantine and Latin periods.

Over the doorway into the esonarthex is a figure of the Virgin and Child. At the entrance to the diakonikon, on the south side, are a mosaic figure of the Archangel Michael and, to the east of this, another representation of the Mother of God Kyriotissa. The mosaic of Jesus in the Temple between the apse of the pre-Iconoclastic church and older masonry dates from the 7th–8th c., making it the earliest of its kind in Istanbul. In the northern apsidiole of the diakonikon are fragments of a cycle of frescoes on the life of St Francis of Assisi. Painted between 1227 and 1260, these are among the earliest paintings of the Saint.

Kanlı Kilise C4
(Church of the Panaghia Mouchliotissa; St Mary of the Mongols)

Location
Near Sancaktar Yokuşu

Bus stop
Fener

This church, still in the hands of the Greek Orthodox Church, was founded in the 13th c. by Isaac Ducas. About 1282 Maria Palaeologina, daughter of the Emperor Michael VIII and widow of the Mongol Khan Abagu, became a nun in the convent here under the name of Melane. Hence the name of the church, St Mary of the Mongols; the Turkish name probably comes from khan, corrupted into the form kanlı (red).

Architecturally the church is notable for its quatrefoil plan. The central dome is borne on four columns. Each of the four conches has three niches.

The church contains a fine mosaic icon of the Virgin and Child.

Kapalı Çarşı (Covered Bazaar, Great Bazaar)   D6/7

The Great Bazaar covers an extensive area between the Nuruosmaniye Mosque and the University quarter. In this labyrinth of almost 90 dimly lit lanes, most of them roofed over, enclosed by a wall with several gates, there are more than 3500 shops and booths offering an extraordinary variety of goods. These range from the cheapest junk to valuable antiques (though these are now rare). Other shops are found in open streets extending north to the Golden Horn. Also included in the complex are a mosque, restaurants and cafés, banks, information bureaux, drinking-fountains and lavatories.
The opening times are Monday to Saturday, 8 a.m. to 7 p.m. Closed on Sunday and public holidays.

Location
Between Nuruosmaniye and Beyazit Mosques

Main entrances
Hürriyet Meydanı/
Beyazit Mosque
Çemberlitaş/
Nuruosmaniye Mosque

The Bazaar can probably trace its origins to the ancient bread market (Artopolion) which lay a little to the south of the present Great Bazaar. In 1461 Mehmet the Conqueror built the Eski Bedesten (Old Market), which still survives in the heart of the complex, and this was enlarged by Süleyman the Magnificent. The Bazaar was badly damaged by fire in 1651, 1791 and 1954 and by earthquake tremors in 1894, but on each occasion was rebuilt.

History

This vaulted hall with 15 domes is the core of the Great Bazaar. Here are to be found the dealers in old weapons and antiques.

Eski Bedesten
(Old Market)

Jewellers in the Great Bazaar

Kapalı Çarşı

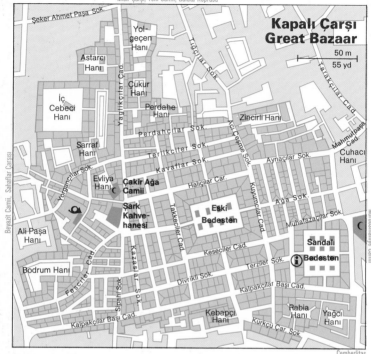

Mısır Çarşı, Yeni Camii, Galata Köprüsü

Kapalı Çarşı
Great Bazaar

50 m
55 yd

Şeker Ahmet Paşa Sok.

Çemberlitaş

Sandalı Bedesten	At the south-east corner of the Bazaar, near the Nuruosmaniye Mosque, is the Sandalı Bedesten, with 20 domes, which was probably established in the time of Mehmet the Conqueror. Auctions which attract many bidders are held here on Monday and Thursday afternoons.
Sahaflar Çarşısı	Immediately adjoining the Beyazit Mosque, the Sahaflar Çarşısı is a paradise for the book-hunter with its large arrays of second-hand books old and new.
Bitpazarı (Flea Market)	The Bitpazarı (Flea Market) is also near the Beyazit Mosque. Here a great range of curious and unlikely articles are offered for sale.

Kara Deniz (Black Sea)

Situation	The Black Sea, known in antiquity as the Pontus Euxinus, lies to the north-east of the Aegean and Mediterranean, linked with them by the Bosphorus (see Boğaziçi), Sea of Marmara (see

In the Covered Bazaar ▶

Marmara Denizi) and Dardanelles (see Çanakkale Boğazı). It is separated from the Sea of Azov (area c. 22,500 sq. km (8700 sq. miles)) to the north by the Crimea.

Extent

The Black Sea covers an area of some 460,000 sq. km (178,000 sq. miles) and contains some 500,000 cu. km (120,000 cu. miles) of water. It extends for about 1150 km (715 miles) from east to west and at its widest point some 600 km (375 miles) from north to south. Three of Europe's most important rivers – the Danube, the Dnieper and the Don – flow into the Black Sea, and the following States border on it: Turkey (ports Zonguldak, Samsun and Trabzon), Bulgaria (Varna), Romania (Constanţa) and the Soviet Union (Odessa, Sevastopol, Yalta and Batumi).

Geology

The basin of the Black Sea, which has a maximum depth of 2240 (7350 ft), was formed only in the Late Tertiary era and has been subject until quite recent times to morphological changes, as the raised beaches on the coast of Thrace and Asia Minor demonstrate.

Water

As a result of the considerable inflow of fresh water from rivers the water of the Black Sea has a relatively low salt content. In the surface levels it amounts to about 1·8 per cent, rising to a maximum of 2·3 per cent at greater depths. The temperature range at the surface is unusually high: in February the minimum can be as low as +6 °C (43 °F), while in August temperatures of around +30 °C (86 °F) have been recorded. On the bottom a constant temperature of +9 °C (48 °F) prevails. The resultant sharp stratification of the water of the Black Sea combines with the barrier effect of the higher bed of the Bosphorus and the strong surface current from the Black Sea through the Bosphorus to the Sea of Marmara to prevent any seasonal redistribution between different levels, and this in turn leads, from a depth of about 200 m (650 ft), to loss of oxygen and a rapid increase in hydrogen sulphide content: hence the name Black Sea.

Beaches

All round the Black Sea there are good bathing beaches. The most popular beaches within easy reach of Istanbul are at Kilyos in Thrace and Şile in Anatolia.

---

* * Kariye Camii (Church of St Saviour in Chora)   C3

Location
Kariye Camii Sok.

Bus stop
Edirnekapı

Opening times
Wed.–Mon. 9.30 a.m.–
4.30 p.m.

Admission charge

Charge for photography

The Church of St Saviour in Chora is one of the most important Byzantine monuments in Istanbul, world-famous for its mosaics and frescoes of the period of the Palaeologue Renaissance (13th–14th c.).

The date of foundation and the original dedication of the church and monastery are not certainly established. Some scholars regard a foundation in the 5th c. as probable. Considerable parts of the present church were built in the late 11th c. by Maria Ducaena, mother-in-law of the Emperor Alexius Comnenus. About 1120 the church was repaired after an earthquake by her grandson Isaac Comnenus.

At the turn of the 13th and 14th c. Theodore Metochites, Grand Logothete (the highest Imperial official) to the Emperor Andronicus II, carried out large-scale rebuilding and

Byzantine mosaics . . .

. . . in the Kariye Camii

111

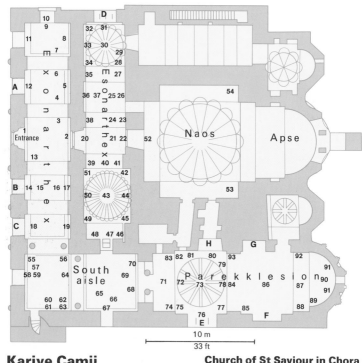

Kariye Camii

Church of St Saviour in Chora

Mosaics

EXONARTHEX
 1 Mother of God with angels
 2 Christ Pantocrator
 3 Marriage feast at Cana
 4 Temptation of Christ
 5 Nativity
 6 Christ's meeting with John
 7 Christ and John
 8 Enrolment for taxation
 9 Jesus in the Temple
 10 Joseph's dream
 11 The 12-year-old Jesus on the way to Jerusalem
 12 Return of the Holy Family from Egypt
 13 Multiplication of the loaves
 14 Flight of Elizabeth and John
 15 (unidentified)
 16 Healing of the leper
 17 The Three Kings before Herod
 18 Mourning mothers
 19 Herod consults the priests and scribes

ESONARTHEX
 20 Mary is given the purple wool
 21 Presentation in the Temple
 22 Christ with Theodore Metochites
 23 Peter
 24 The Virgin's first steps
 25 The caresses
 26 Birth of the Virgin
 27 Joachim and Anne at the Golden Gate
 28 Joachim
 29 Annunciation to Anne
 30 Mother of God
 31 Scene (unidentified) from the life of the Virgin
 32 Rejection of Joachim's offerings
 33 Joseph's departure
 34 Annunciation to the Virgin
 35 Joseph and Mary
 36 Betrothal of Mary and Joseph
 37 Blessing by the priests
 38 Zacharias' prayer

 39 The Virgin in the Temple school
 40 The Virgin fed by angels
 41 Paul
 42 Healing of Peter's mother-in-law
 43 Christ Pantocrator with his ancestors
 44 Deesis, with Isaac Comnenus and Melane
 45 Healing of the woman with a bloody flux
 46 (unidentified)
 47 Healing of the withered hand
 48 Healing of the leper
 49 Healing of the blind man and the dumb man
 50 Healing of the sick
 51 Healing of the two blind men

NAOS
 52 Dormition of the Mother of God
 53 Mother of God with Child

Kariye Camii

redecoration, adorning the church with its superb mosaics and frescoes.

At the end of the 15th c. the church was converted into a mosque by Atik Ali Paşa, Sultan Beyazit II's Grand Vizier. In the 19th c. it became necessary to rebuild the central dome and the dome over the diakonikon.

Between 1947 and 1958 experts from the Byzantine Institute of America uncovered and restored the surviving Byzantine mosaics and frescoes. The Kariye Camii is now open to the public as a museum.

54 Christ with book

SOUTH AISLE
55 Christ and the woman of Samaria
56 Healing of the lame man
57 (unidentified)
58 Massacre of the Innocents
59 (unidentified)
60 Healing of the man with a palsy
61 Massacre of the Innocents
62 Healing of the man with dropsy
63 Healing of the blind
64 (unidentified)
65 (unidentified)
66 Calling of Zacchaeus
67 Flight into Egypt
68 (unidentified)
69 (unidentified)
70 Return of the Three Kings

Frescoes
PAREKKLESION
71 Souls of the righteous
72 Melchizedek
73 Mother of God with angels
74 The angel protecting the city of Jerusalem
75 Hymnographer
76 Consecration of the Temple
77 Hymnographer
78 Christ
79 Hymnographer
80 The Burning Bush
81 Jacob's fight with the angel
82 Hymnographer
83 Aaron and his sons
84 Christ
85 Consecration of the Temple
86 Last Judgment
87 Michael
88 Raising of Jairus' daughter
89 Mother of God Eleousa

90 Anastasis
91 Fathers of the Church
92 Raising of the widow's son
93 Moses and the Burning Bush

Tombs
EXONARTHEX
A (unidentified)
B (unidentified)
C Princess Irene Palaeologina

ESONARTHEX
D Demetrius Ducas Angelus Palaeologus

PAREKKLESION
E Michael Tomikes
F (unidentified)
G (unidentified)
H Theodore Metochites

Kariye Camii

Architecture

The church is built in alternating courses of brick and stone and has five domes carried on drums with round-headed windows. The cruciform naos under the principal dome perpetuates the ground-plan of Maria Ducaena's domed cruciform church. The apse, roofed with a semi-dome, has an arch borne on pillars. At the west end are an esonarthex with two domes and an exonarthex. At the south-west corner of the exonarthex is the former bell-tower, converted into a minaret. On the south side of the naos is the parekklesion; on the north side is a two-storey annexe.

Mosaics

The magnificent mosaics of the Kariye Camii are master works of the Palaeologue Renaissance. Almost completely preserved in the two narthexes and fragmentarily preserved in the main church, they cover a wide range of subjects, from the ancestors of Christ to the Last Judgment. The finest of the mosaics are the "Mother of God with Angels" above the entrance doorway, "Christ Pantocrator" over the door into the esonarthex, "Christ enthroned" with the founder, Theodore Metochites, over the door into the naos and a "Deesis" with Isaac Comnenus and the nun Melane on the east wall of the esonarthex.

Frescoes

In the parekklesion, which served as a burial chapel, are a unique series of frescoes on the theme of death, resurrection and life after death. The high points of this cycle are the dome-painting of the Virgin and Child surrounded by angels, the Last Judgment in the bay between the apse and the naos and the Anastasis (Resurrection) on the wall of the apse.

---

*Kılıç Ali Paşa Camii (Kılıç Ali Paşa Mosque)   C8

Location
Necati Bey Cad./Tophane
İskele Cad.

Bus stop
Tophane

This mosque on the west side of the Bosphorus, founded by Admiral Kılıç Ali Paşa in 1580 and built by Sinan, is one of the most interesting buildings of its kind. Evidently influenced by Byzantine architecture, Sinan followed not only the ground-plan of Haghia Sophia but also the structure of its vaulting. The mosque resembles a Christian church in having a central area divided into aisles by columns, galleries and a narthex-like vestibule closed by a grille. The main dome and the surrounding half-domes are supported on four "elephants' feet".
The tiled decoration of the interior, particularly the mihrab, is very beautiful. There are also fine capitals and marble-work. The prayer hall is floored with tiles of particular beauty.
In the mosque garden is the türbe of the founder, octagonal in plan with a T-shaped interior.
The hamam (bath-house), also designed by Sinan, is on a hexagonal plan.

---

*Kızıl Adalar (Princes' Islands)

Location
19–28 km (12–17 miles)
SSE of Istanbul

Boat services
Several times daily to and
from Istanbul and Yalova

One of the most attractive outings from Istanbul is a boat trip to the beautiful Princes' Islands at the north-eastern end of the Sea of Marmara. Carefully tended gardens and parks, excellent facilities for water-sports and good roads and pathways provide welcome relief from the stresses of city life.
There are no cars on the islands: the main form of transport is horse-drawn carriages, much used by visitors for trips about the islands.

114

Fishing harbour on Burgaz Ada

Horse-carriage, Burgaz Ada

Burgaz Ada (Greek Pyrgos or Antigoni)

This island of varied scenery probably takes its name from a tower which formerly stood on its highest point (165 m (541 ft). The island's water-sports facilities and its excellent and well-maintained roads and footpaths (excursions by horse-carriage) attract large numbers of visitors. Near the Greek Orthodox church is a house once occupied by the famous Turkish poet Sait Faik (1907–54), now a museum (open Tues.–Sat. 9 a.m. to 5 p.m.).

Büyük Ada (Greek Prinkipo)

This "island of pines", the largest and most populous in the group, is now a major summer resort, with fine villas, clubs, hotels and a wide range of recreational facilities which cater for hosts of visitors.

On İsa Tepe, a hill at the north end of the island (163 m (535 ft), is the Monastery of the Transfiguration, and on Yüce Tepe (201 m (659 ft)), at the south end, the fortress-like Monastery of St George, from the terrace of which there are fine panoramic views.

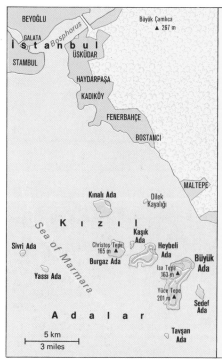

Princes' Islands
Kızıl Adalar

The nine **Princes' Islands** which lie in the Sea of Marmara between 12 and 17 miles south-east of Istanbul, are known in Turkish as **Kızıl Adalar**, the Red Islands, from the colouring of the rock (quartzite and ironstone) of which their hills are formed. Their healthy climate, southern vegetation and varied scenery make them a favourite resort of the more prosperous citizens of Istanbul.

In antiquity the islands were known as the Demonnesoi (People's Islands), in the Middle Ages as Papadonisia (Priests' Islands) on account of their numerous monasteries. Under the Byzantine Emperors they were frequently used as a place of exile for unwanted members of the Imperial Family.

The largest of the islands, in Turkish **Büyük Ada** (Great Island), was known from the time of Justin II (6th c.) as Prinkipo: hence the present name of these islands. The other islands, in order of size, with Greek names in brackets, are Heybeli Ada (Chalki), Burgaz Ada (Pyrgos or Antigoni), Kınalı Ada (Proti), Sedef Ada (Terebinthos), Yassı Ada (Plati), Sivri Ada (Oxia), Kaşık Ada (Pitta) and Tavşan Ada (Neandros).

Heybeli Ada (Greek Chalki)

The Greek name of this island comes from the copper mined here (remains of a mine in the Bay of Çamlimanı on the south side of the island). Heybeli Ada is now the seat of the Turkish Naval Academy (in the bay in front of the Academy is the "Savarona", once Atatürk's private yacht).

In the saddle between two hills at the north end of the island is the former Theological Seminary of the Orthodox Church. On the hill to the west stands the only surviving Byzantine church on the Princes' Islands (15th c.; quatrefoil plan); permission to visit it can be obtained from the Commandant of the Naval Academy.

Kınalı Ada (Greek Proti)

Kıınalı Ada, the island nearest Istanbul, has a number of small bathing beaches. There are three ruined monasteries, once used as places of internment for exiled members of the Imperial House. From the island's highest point (115 m (377 ft)) there are beautiful panoramic views.

Sivri Ada (Greek Oxia)

This crag of rock rising out of the sea to a height of 90 m (295 ft) is notable only for the fact that in 1911 thousands of ownerless dogs which had been rounded up in the street of Istanbul were marooned here and left to starve.

*Kız Kulesi (Maiden's Tower; Leander's Tower)   C11

The 30 m (100 ft) high tower known as Leander's Tower, on a rocky islet off the Asiatic shore of the Bosphorus, is one of Istanbul's best-known landmarks. In its present form it dates from 1763.

The Turkish name of Kız Kulesi, or Maiden's Tower, comes from the legend of a Sultan's daughter who, it had been prophesied, would die of snakebite. She lived in this isolated tower, thinking that she would be safe there, but died of a bite from a snake which found its way to the little islet in a basket of fruit. The name by which the tower is commonly known comes from the story of Hero and Leander, though in fact the setting of that story was the Dardanelles (see Çanakkale Boğazı) and not the Bosphorus (see Boğaziçi).

There is believed to have been a toll-station on the islet about 500 B.C. The Byzantines built a small fort here, from which at a later stage an iron chain was stretched across the Bosphorus. In 1545 the fort was completely rebuilt and equipped with cannon. In 1721 its wooden tower was burned down, and in 1763 the present Baroque tower was built. It is now used as a signal station and control post.

Location
180 m (200 yd) off the Asiatic shore of the Bosphorus at Salacak

Boats
From Salacak İskelesi

Kıztası (Maiden's Column; Column of Marcian) D4

Location
Kıztası Cad.

Bus stop
Fâtih

As an inscription on its base indicates, this column was erected by the City Prefect, Tatianus, in the mid 5th c. in honour of the Emperor Marcian.

The column, of pink granite, is just under 9 m (30 ft) high. It stands on a marble base with the remains of fine relief sculpture. Originally it probably carried the Imperial coat of arms, as the eagles at the corners of the plinth suggest.

The Turkish name of Maiden's Column relates to legends which grew up round the reliefs on the base. The column was credited with the ability to distinguish true from pretended virginity.

*Küçük Ayasofya (Little Haghia Sophia; Church of SS. Sergius and Bacchus E7

Location
Mehmet Paşa Sok.

Bus stop
Sultanahmet

Little Haghia Sophia, originally a Byzantine church, stands on a site charged with history. Immediately adjoining it there once stood the Palace of Hormizdas, named after a Sassanid prince who sought refuge at the Court of Constantine the Great. A basilica dedicated to SS. Peter and Paul was built within the precincts of the palace about 518, and some years later the Church of SS. Sergius and Bacchus was erected on the north side of this church, sharing a common vestibule with it. About the year 536 the Palace of Hormizdas was converted into a monastery, of which the Empress Theodora was a munificent patroness.

Küçük Ayasofya

At the beginning of the 16th c. the Turks converted the church, which had become a much-frequented place of pilgrimage on account of its great store of relics, into a mosque, which involved considerable changes in the vestibule and the interior. Further changes were made in the 18th and 19th c. The building is at present in course of restoration.

Crown of principal dome

The Byzantine Church of SS. Sergius and Bacchus, which some authorities have seen as the model for San Vitale in Ravena and Charlemagne's Palatine Chapel in Aachen, is a building of great architectural interest, with a domed octagon enclosed within an irregular rectangle. At the corners of the octagon are niches roofed with semi-domes. The two-storey aisles are separated from the nave by columns. The apse projects at the east end. The main dome is divided into 16 compartments lit by windows, eight of them concave and eight flat. The minaret is built against the south-west corner of the former narthex.

The spatial effect of the church can best be appreciated from the gallery opposite the choir apse. The green and red marble columns (marble from Synnada in Thessaly), with melon capitals on the ground floor and pseudo-Ionic capitals in the gallery, the ornamentation and the recently exposed remains of marble facing and mosaics bear witness to the former splendours of the Church of SS. Sergius and Bacchus. In a frieze above the lower order of columns is the foundation inscription, written in hexameters.

The Islamic furnishings are oriented towards Mecca, at an angle to the axis of the building. Between the windows in the principal dome are monogram-like calligraphic inscriptions.

Küçük Ayasofya: capital

Tulip Mosque: interior

*Küçüksu

Location
11 km (7 miles) NE of city centre

Bus stop
Küçüksu

Boat landing-stage
Küçüksu

A little way south of the point where the Sweet Waters of Asia flow into the Bosphorus is Küçüksu, much esteemed as a summer resort in Ottoman times. Its principal attraction is the elegant Rococo palace built by the architect Nikoğos Balyan for Sultan Abdül Mecit I in 1856–57. Near the palace is a beautiful Baroque fountain erected by Valide Sultan Mihrişah in 1796. To the south of the boat landing-stage stands the Kıbrıslı Yalısı, one of the largest seaside mansions on the Bosphorus, built in 1760 and subsequently much altered, with superb marble decoration. Near by is the Kırmızı Yalı (Red Mansion), perhaps the most beautiful yalı on the Bosphorus, which was built at the end of the 18th c. by a well-to-do family of French and Polish extraction.

Kyriotissa Church

See Kalenderhane Camii

*Lâleli Camii (Tulip Mosque) D5

Location
Ordu Cad., Aksaray

The Tulip Mosque was built for Sultan Mustafa III in 1763; the architect is believed to have been Mehmet Tahir. Two years later it was destroyed by an earthquake, but it was rebuilt by

Tulip Mosque

1783. In Baroque style, it stands on a massive vaulted substructure within which is a hall containing a fountain and surrounded by shops. It is flanked by two minarets, each with a single balcony.

The central dome rests on an octagonal drum borne on columns. Against the entrance and mihrab sides of the dome are six semi-domes. The mihrab and the handsome Sultan's loge (on the left) are given added dignity by columned galleries.

More than a hundred windows, many of them with vivid stained glass, admit an abundance of light and illuminate the porphyry facing of the walls.

Adjoining the mosque is the türbe of the founder and his murdered son Selim III. The medrese which formed part of the complex has been preserved; the bath-house (hamam) has not.

Bus stop
Lâleli

**Land Walls

A–F1–3

The land walls of Constantinople, the mightiest fortifications of Late Antiquity, extend from the Golden Horn to the Sea of Marmara, with a total length of 6670 m (7295 yd).

Location
W side of city

Theodosian Walls

The Theodosian Walls, constructed in the first half of the 5th c., form the main part of the land walls. This triple belt of fortifications (moat, outer and inner walls), with a width of some 60 m (200 ft), gave the city complete protection against enemy attack until the introduction of firearms and artillery.

The moat was some 18 m (59 ft) wide and 6–7 m (20–23 ft) deep. The outer wall had 96 towers 10 m (33 ft) high; the main (inner) wall also had 96, 15–20 m (50–65 ft) in height.

The Edirne Gate, the most northerly gate in the Theodosian Walls, was originally one of the most important. Through this gate the Emperors Justinian I and Leo V entered Constantinople. Only scanty remains of the gate, which was destroyed in 1453, are still to be seen. Near the gate is Tekfur Sarayı (see entry).

Edirne Kapısı (Edirne Gate)

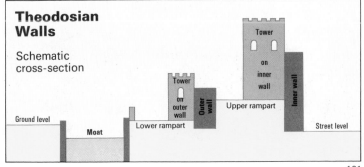

Theodosian Walls

Schematic cross-section

Tower

on inner wall

Tower

on outer wall

Upper rampart

Ground level

Moat

Lower rampart

Street level

Outer wall

Inner wall

A section of the Theodosian Walls

Remains of the land walls at Tekfur Sarayı

A gardener at work in the old moat   *Topkapı*

The Sulukule Gate, in the Lycus Valley, is also badly damaged; its outwork is completely destroyed.

Sulukule Kapısı
(Sulukule Gate)

Topkapı (Cannon Gate), known in Byzantine times as the Gate of St Romanus, featured prominently in the Turkish siege of 1453. It was rebuilt by the Turks after its destruction. It is now the main entrance to Istanbul from the west.

Topkapı

This is the best-preserved gate in the Theodosian Walls. With its outer and inner gate it gives a good impression of the fortification techniques of the 5th c.

Mevlevihane Kapısı

The Silivri Gate, also known in Byzantine times as the Gate of the Spring, is near the İbrahim Paşa Mosque. Much altered in the course of its history, it is now typically Turkish in style.

Silivri Kapısı (Silivri Gate)

The Belgrade Gate has features characteristic of late Byzantine military engineering. It was walled up in the time of the Emperor Isaac Angelus and reopened only in 1886.

Belgrat Kapısı
(Belgrade Gate)

See Yedikule

Altın Kapısı (Golden Gate)

The octagonal Marble Tower, directly on the coast, is all that remains of a fort of the time of Basil II. It stands at the junction of the land walls and the sea walls along the Sea of Marmara.

Mermerkule (Marble Tower)

Blachernae Walls

The Theodosian Walls are continued northward by the older Blachernae Walls, which originally enclosed the Blachernae quarter of the city. On account of the fall in the ground here there was only a single line of walls, with the towers set closer together. Only scanty remains survive, for example in the substructures of the Blachernae Palace (see Tekfur Sarayı) and at the Eğri Kapı, the Crooked Gate (the old Porta Caligaria). The massive towers of Isaac Angelus and Anemas combine with the walls to support the terrace of the Palace.

Wall of Heraclius

The 7th c. Wall of Heraclius, which extended into the marshy zone on the shore of the Golden Horn, is now difficult to identify.

Leander's Tower

See Kız Kulesi

Little Haghia Sophia

See Küçük Ayasofya

Maiden's Tower

See Kız Kulesi

Marcian, Column of

See Kıztaşı

Maritime Museum

See Deniz Müzesi

Marmara Denizi (Sea of Marmara; Propontis)

The Sea of Marmara (280 km (175 miles) long, up to 80 km (50 miles) wide, up to 1355 m (4445 ft) deep; area 11,352 sq. km (4383 sq. miles)) lies between the Bosphorus (see Boğaziçi) and the Dardanelles (see Çanakkale Boğazı), separating European Turkey from Asia Minor. It came into being in the Early Quaternary era as a rift valley, and its northern part, going down to considerable depths (much of it over

1000 m (3280 ft), down to 1350 m (4430 ft)), is the most westerly element in a sequence of grabens and basins some 1000 km (620 miles) long which plays an important part in the geology of northern Anatolia. From the shallow zone (under 50 m (165 ft)) along the northern coast there emerge the Princes' Islands (see Kızıl Adalar), formed of hard quartzites which have resisted erosion. In the shallow southern part of the sea are a number of islands, including the island of Marmara. The Sea of Marmara, a typical example of an inter-continental sea, lies wholly within the territory of Turkey.

Mehmet Fâtih Mosque

See Sultan Mehmet Fâtih Külliye

Mesih Mehmet Paşa Camii (Mesih Mehmet Paşa Mosque)   C4

This mosque was built by Mesih Mehmet Paşa, Sultan Murat III's Grand Vizier, in 1586. Its architecture is characteristic of the school of Sinan. Rectangular in plan, it has a central dome surrounded by five semi-domes, one of them over the projecting mihrab. On either side of the main dome are side chambers, each with three domes.

The mihrab and mimber are of beautifully worked marble, and the mihrab has superb coloured tiles, mainly floral patterns. Above the windows in the wall opposite the mihrab are tiles with Koranic texts.

The five domes over the vestibule are borne on six porphyry columns.

In front of the mosque are three ablution fountains with marble-faced façades. In the courtyard is the türbe of the founder.

Location
Aksemsettin Cad.,
Karagümrük

Bus stop
Yavuzselim

*Mihrimah Camii (Mihrimah Mosque)   C3

This mosque, also known as the Edirnekapısı Camii (Mosque at the Edirne Gate), is said to have been built by Mihrimah, daughter of Süleyman I and wife of Rüstem Pasa, about 1555. It is attributed to the great architect Sinan. The mosque was badly damaged in two earthquakes in the 18th and late 19th c.; it was restored in 1910 and again in the 1960s.

The main dome, over the square central area, is no less than 37 m (121 ft) high. It is borne on four tower-like corner piers roofed with small domes. The interior is flooded with light from the windows within the three arches on each wall, in the upper arches supporting the dome, the dome itself and the kıbla wall. The mihrab and mimber are in finely worked marble. The painting in the interior is 19th c.

The vestibule is roofed with seven domes. There is a single minaret.

Location
Fevzi Paşa Cad., Edirnekapı

Bus stop
Edirnekapı

Military Museum

See Askeri Müzesi

The Egyptian or Spice Bazaar

*Mısır Çarşısı (Egyptian Bazaar; Spice Bazaar) D7

This L-shaped vaulted building is part of the külliye of the New Mosque (see Yeni Cami), the building of which was sponsored by Turhan Hatice Sultan, mother of Mehmet IV. The bazaar, built in 1660 under the direction of the architect Kasım Ağa, took over the function of a food and spice market established in Byzantine times.

Around the Egyptian Bazaar are numbers of establishments dealing in foodstuffs, both wholesale and retail. Here buyers and sellers meet and conduct their business in a busy and colourful setting.

The various aromas coming from coffee-roasting shops, tea-houses and spice-dealers' establishments mingle here to give the Egyptian Bazaar its own incomparable atmosphere.

Location
Yeni Cami/Hasırcılar Cad.

Main entrance
At Yeni Cami

Bus stop
Eminönü

Opening times
Mon.–Sat. 8 a.m.–7 p.m.;
closed Sun. and public
holidays

Molla Çelebi Camii (Molla Çelebi Mosque) B9

This little mosque was built by Sinan in 1589 for a judge named Molla Çelebi Mehmet Efendi. It has a central dome borne on four columns and surrounded by five semi-domes.

The five-domed vestibule was renovated in 1958, when the relief decoration was also restored. The fountain facing it, by

Location
Meclisi Mebusan Cad.

Bus stop
Kabataş

◀ *Mihrimah Mosque*

the Baroque sculptor Koca Yusuf Paşa (1786), stood until 1958 immediately in front of the mosque.

A hamam (bath-house) which stood in the gardens in front of the mosque (to the right) was removed in 1958.

Mosaic Museum

See Arasta Mozaik Müzesi

Municipal Museum

See Belediye Müzesi

*Murat Paşa Camii (Murat Paşa Mosque)   D4

Location
Vatan Cad./Millet Cad.

Bus stop
Aksaray

This mosque, built of alternating courses of brick and stone, was founded in 1466 by Has Murat Paşa, one of Mehmet the Conqueror's Viziers. It was restored in 1945, with a new mihrab and mimber, but lost its original decoration.

The mosque preserves features characteristic of the earliest Ottoman architecture. It has a T-shaped ground-plan, with two domed central squares, one of these being flanked by two smaller domed rooms on each side. The two imposing main domes are borne on a massive arch.

Murat Paşa Mosque

Nuruosmaniye Mosque

128

The five domes of the vestibule are supported on six columns, two of pink granite and four of verd antique. The minaret, of unusually large diameter, has an air of great massiveness.

Museum of the Ancient Orient

See Arkeoloji Müzesi, Eski Şark Eserleri Müzesi

Museum of Modern Art

See Resim ve Heykel Müzesi

Museum of Turkish and Islamic Art

See Türk ve Islâm Eserleri Müzesi

New Mosque

See Yeni Cami

Nicaea

See İznik

---

*Nuruosmaniye Camii (Mosque of the Sacred Light of Osman)   D7

The Nuruosmaniye, Istanbul's first Baroque mosque, was built by Sultan Mahmut I in 1748–56, the principal architect being Simon Kalfa. This single-domed mosque stands on a high substructure, to which marble steps give access. The massive arches supporting the dome, the great semicircular tympana with their numerous windows and the pilasters are all characteristically Baroque features.

Location
Between Çarşıkapı Sok. and Vezir Hanı Cad., opposite Cağaloğlu Gate of Covered Bazaar

Bus stop
Çemberlitaş

Notable features of the interior are the marble mihrab and the mimber of green porphyry. The imposing cornice and the Sultan's loge are reminiscent of Sinan's later buildings. The horseshoe-shaped courtyard is an innovation. The vestibule has the traditional five domes, but the obligatory ablution fountain is missing. Terminating the north end of the courtyard are nine domed pavilions with porphyry columns.

Between the courtyard and the mosque are two minarets, each with two balconies. The mosque complex also includes a medrese, a public kitchen, a fountain and a library which contains valuable manuscripts.

Nusretiye Camii

Nusretiye Mosque

Nusretiye Camii (Mosque of Victory) C8

Location
Meclisi Mebusan Cad.,
Tophane

Bus stop
Tophane

The Nusretiye Mosque was built by the Armenian architect Kirkor Balyan in 1822–26 for Sultan Mahmut II, replacing an earlier mosque of the time of Selim III which had been destroyed by fire. This monumental single-domed mosque, flanked by elegant minarets with two balconies, combines Baroque and Empire features. Charmingly decorative additions are the balustrades over the cornices of the arches supporting the dome and the bulbous vases topping the pilasters round the dome.

The interior has fine calligraphic inscriptions (gilt on marble) by the celebrated calligrapher Kazaskar Mustafa Rakum Efendi, completed after his death by Sakir Efendi. Other notable features are the marble mimber and mihrab, the elegant bronze grilles closing off the Sultan's loge and the steps leading up to the platform with the ablution fountain. Note also the drinking-fountain and the clock-room (muvakkithane).

Old Seraglio

See Topkapı Sarayı

Opera House

See Taksim Meydanı

Ortaköy Camii

The Ortaköy Mosque was built by Sultan Abdül Mecit in 1854. The site – then far outside the city – had previously been occupied by a mosque founded by Mahmut Ağa and Mehmet Ağa.

Location
European side of Bosphorus, near Ortaköy Iskelesi

This single-domed mosque in neo-Baroque style, designed by Nikoğos Balyan, is of striking effect with its massive corner piers and two unusually slender minarets. It was damaged by an earthquake in 1894.

Bus stop
Ortaköy

Boat landing-stage
Ortaköy

The interior walls are faced with white and red marble mosaic panels. The mihrab, mimber and Kuran kürsü are decorated with porphyry.

Pammakaristos Monastery

See Fethiye Camii

Pantocrator Monastery

See Zeyrek Camii

Pera

See Beyoğlu

Piyer Loti (Pierre Loti)

See Eyüp

Princes' Islands

See Kızıl Adalar

Prince's Mosque

See Şehzade Camii

Propontis

See Marmara Denizi

Resim ve Heykel Müzesi (Museum of Modern Art)　　B10/11

Location
Dolmabahçe Sarayı

Bus stops
Dolmabahçe, Beşiktaş

This collection of works by modern Turkish artists is housed in the Veliaht Apartments of Dolmabahçe Sarayı (see entry). Note particularly the works by Osman Nuri, Salih Molla Aski and Hüseyin Giritli (Primitivists); Şeker Ahmed Paşa, Osman Hamdi and Ahmed Ziya (members of the Second Generation group); and İbrahim Calli, Feyhaman Duran, Ali Riza, Namik İsmail and Hikmet Onat (Impressionists).
The museum also contains collections of folk-art and ceramics.

Revolution, Museum of the

See Atatürk Müzesi

Rose Mosque

See Gül Camii

Roxelana's Baths

See Haseki Hürrem Hamamı

Rumeli Hisarı, guarding the Bosphorus

Roxelana, Türbe of

See Sultan Süleyman I Külliye

*Rumeli Hisarı (Fortress)

The Fortress of Rumeli Hisarı is the mightiest of the strong-
holds along the Bosphorus, and is situated at its narrowest
point (660 m (720 yd)). It is now the setting of open-air
performances and *son et lumière* shows in summer.

Built on the steep European shore of the Bosphorus, Rumeli
Hisarı is defended by stout walls and massive round towers
(three large and 13 smaller ones; walls up to 7 m (23 ft) thick)
and fortified gates.

The fortress lost its function soon after it was built, when the
Turks took Constantinople. Thereafter it was used for a time as
a State prison. After extensive renovation it was opened to the
public as a museum in 1959.

Location
European side of Bosphorus,
15 km (9 miles) from city
centre

Bus stop
Rumeli Hisarı

Boat landing-stage
Rumeli Hisarı

Opening times
Tues.–Sun. 9.30 a.m.–
4.30 p.m.

Kilyos, Sariyer

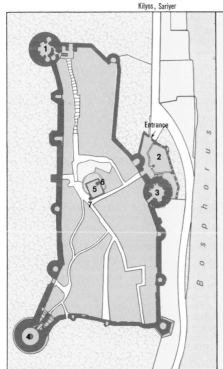

Rumeli Hisarı

1 Sarıca Paşa Kulesi
2 Barbican
3 Halil Paşa Kulesi
4 Zaganos Paşa Kulesi
5 Mosque
6 Cistern
7 Minaret

The fortress of **Rumeli Hisarı** was
built by Mehmet the Conqueror in
1451–52. Situated on the European
shore of the Bosphorus at its narrowest point, it was designed, along
with the Fortress of Anadolu Hisarı on
the Asiatic side, to control the straits.
After the capture of Constantinople
by the Turks both fortresses lost their
raison d'être.

It was probably at this point that the
Persian King Darius I, in 512 B.C., built
a bridge of boats over the Bosphorus
– an early predecessor of the modern
suspension bridge which now spans
the Bosphorus farther to the south. It
is planned to build a second bridge
over the Bosphorus at Rumeli Hisarı.

50 m
55 yd

The massive walls of Rumeli Hisarı

Rumeli Kavağı

See Boğaziçi

*Rüstem Paşa Camii (Rüstem Paşa Mosque)   D7

Location
Ragıp Gümüşpala Cad.

Bus stop
Eminönü

Boat landing-stage
Eminönü

This mosque, one of the most beautiful in Istanbul, was built by Sinan in 1560 for Rüstem Paşa, Süleyman the Magnificent's Grand Vizier and son-in-law.

The mosque, in the classical style of Ottoman architecture, stands on a massive substructure containing warehouses and shops. At either end flights of steps lead up to the courtyard gardens.

The great dome is borne on eight piers, four free-standing and four built into the north and south walls. At the corners of the square central area are semi-domes. The interior is notable for its magnificent tile decoration. Superbly beautiful tiles cover not only the mihrab and the kıbla wall but also the rear of the mimber and the doorway. Even the upper parts of the columns supporting the dome are faced with tiles. The tiles are in a wide variety of patterns, both floral (tulips, pomegranates, tree and leaf designs) and geometric (spheres, lightning flashes). The tiles in the vestibule are among the finest produced in the second half of the 16th c.

The marble-work is also very fine, and the Kuran kürsü with its beautiful mother-of-pearl inlays is a marvel of Turkish craftsmanship in wood.

Near by, to the south-east, is a medrese built by Sinan for Rüstem Paşa about 1550, with an unusual octagonal courtyard. It is now a students' residence.

St George's Church

See Haghios Georgios

St Mary of the Mongols

See Kanlı Kilise

St Saviour in Chora

See Kariye Camii

SS. Sergius and Bacchus

See Küçük Ayasofya

Rüstem Paşa Mosque

Prince's Mosque

Sandalı Bedesten

See Kapalı Çarşı

Scutari

See Üsküdar

Sea Walls   B-F1-9

Walls on the Sea of Marmara

Location
Seraglio Point to
Mermerkule

The Marmara section of the sea walls runs west above the shore from Seraglio Point to the Mermerkule, where it meets the land walls. Recent investigations have shown that the oldest parts of these walls were probably built as early as the 2nd c. A.D. They were considerably strengthened in the 8th and 9th c. In their final form they stood 12–15 m (40–50 ft) high, with over 180 20 m (65 ft) high towers and eight gates. The best-preserved stretch is between Seraglio Point and the Küçük Ayasofya Camii, in which different building phases can be identified.

Walls on the Golden Horn

Location
Seraglio Point to
Blachernae quarter

The sea walls along the Golden Horn, built from 438 onwards, consist of two sections. One, from Seraglio Point to near the Atatürk Bridge, was destroyed during road construction work in the 1950s. The other, from Atatürk Bridge to the Blachernae quarter, can still be traced.

The walls were originally 5 km (3 miles) long and some 10 m (33 ft) high, with 14 gates and more than 100 towers.

*Şehzade Camii (Prince's Mosque)   D5

Location
Şehzadebaşı Cad.

Bus stop
Şehzade

This mosque was built by Sultan Süleyman the Magnificent in honour of his eldest son, Prince Saruhan Şehzade Mehmet, who died in 1543 at the age of 21. The mosque, completed in 1548, was designed by the great Sinan, who referred to it as his "apprentice work".

Architecture
(see plan and section)
opposite

The mosque, square in plan, follows a clear pattern similar to that of a Byzantine domed cruciform church. Four great "elephant's foot" piers support the main dome (37 m (121 ft) high, 18 m (59 ft) in diameter), surrounded by four semi-domes, which in turn are each flanked by two smaller semi-domes. Seen from outside, the roof is a cascade of domes flowing down from the great central dome to terminate in the tower-like structure at the corners.

Two graceful minarets, each with two balconies, flank the side of the mosque facing the courtyard, which also is square in plan, with domed colonnades (revak) on all four sides.

Prince's Mosque

Şehzade Camii

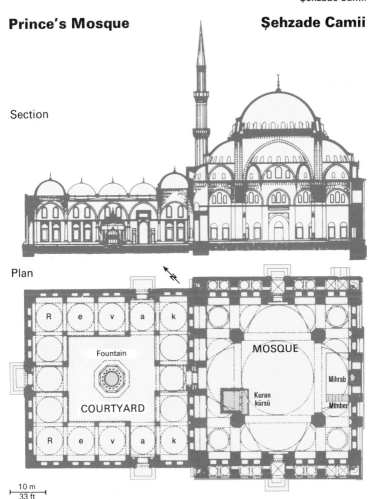

Section

Plan

R e v a k

Fountain

MOSQUE

COURTYARD

Mihrab

Kuran kürsü

Mimber

R e v a k

10 m
33 ft

In contrast to the attractive exterior, the interior appears plain and lacking in decoration. The only exception is the marble mimber, decorated with delicate geometric patterns and reliefs, which is a marvel of its kind.

Interior

In the mosque garden are a number of türbes belonging to relatives of various Sultans. The most beautiful is the octagonal Türbe of Prince Mehmet, the interior of which is decorated with exquisite tiles in the *cuerda seca* technique. Also very fine are

Türbes

the painted decoration of the dome and a canopy of walnut wood inlaid with ivory over the tomb.

Subsidiary buildings

The mosque complex includes a number of other buildings, now converted to other uses. The medrese is at present used as a hostel, while the caravanserai is occupied by research institutes.

Selimiye Camii (Edirne)

See Edirne, Selimiye Camii

Selimiye Camii (Istanbul)

See Sultan Selim I Camii

Seraglio

See Topkapı Sarayı

Serpent Column

See At Meydanı, Burmalı Sütun

Sinan, Türbe of

See Sultan Süleyman I Külliye

Şişli Camii (Şişli Mosque)

Location
Büyükdere Cad.

Bus stop
Şişli

The Şişli Mosque (architect Vasfı Egeli) was built in 1949–54. Designed in classical style, it has a main dome 11·4 m (37 ft) in diameter surrounded by three half-domes. As in many other mosques, the vestibule is roofed with five small domes.
The interior has inscriptions by the contemporary calligraphers Halim, Hamit and Macit. In front of the courtyard is a beautiful ablution fountain, and facing this are a small library and the custodian's lodge.

*Sokullu Mehmet Paşa Camii (Sokullu Mehmet Paşa Mosque)　　E7

Location
Şehit Mehmet Paşa Sok.

Bus stop
Sultanahmet

This charming little mosque was built by Sinan in 1571–72 for İsmihan Sultan, daughter of Selim II and wife of the Grand Vizier, Sokullu Mehmet Paşa. Its great attraction is the exquisite tile decoration of the interior. The mosque occupies the site of the Byzantine Church of St Anastasia.

Built on a rectangular plan, the mosque is crowned by a dome borne on six piers and flanked by two semi-domes on each side, reflecting the architect's original conception of hexagonal plan.

Architecture

The kıbla wall, entirely faced with tiles, is particularly beautiful, and the mihrab itself, of elaborately worked marble, is still further enhanced by its decoration of coloured tiles in floral and foliage designs and its fine calligraphic inscriptions. The conical roof of the mimber is also tiled. Some of the stones set into the mihrab and mimber are said to have come from the Kaaba in Mecca.

Interior

The courtyard, surrounded on three sides by a combination of medrese cells and colonnades, is one of Sinan's finest conceptions. Facing the main doorway of the mosque, on the same axis as the marble ablution fountain with a canopy roof borne on columns, is the domed dershane, the lecture hall of the medrese.

Courtyard

Spice Bazaar

See Mısır Çarşısı

Studius, Monastery of

See İmrahor Camii

Sublime Porte

See Bab-ı Ali

Süleymaniye Camii

See Sultan Süleyman I Külliye

Sultan Ahmet Camii (Sultan Ahmet Mosque, Blue Mosque)

E7/8

The Sultan Ahmet Mosque, widely known as the Blue Mosque, is one of Istanbul's largest and most beautiful mosques. With its pyramidal cascade of domes and semi-domes, its six slender minarets, its mature architectural ornament and its very mass it is a fit counterpart to its neighbour, Haghia Sophia (see Ayasofya).
The mosque was built for Sultan Ahmet I by Mehmet Ağa, a pupil of the great Sinan, and was completed in 1616 after seven years' work.

Location
Sultanahmet

Bus stop
Sultanahmet

From an enclosed outer garden we enter the forecourt of the mosque, which is surrounded by a peristyle of 26 granite columns with stalactitic capitals supporting 30 small domes.

Forecourt

Blue Mosque

Perspective view

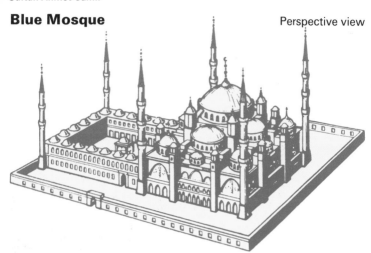

Sultan Ahmet Camii

Plan

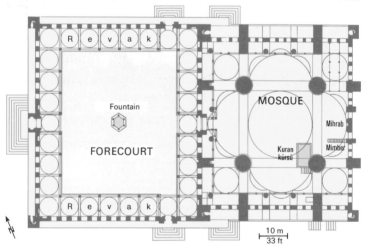

On all three sides are gateways on a monumental scale. In the centre of the courtyard is a hexagonal ablution fountain.
The main gateway, with elaborate stalactitic vaulting, is on the east side of the mosque.

Mosque

The mosque is on a quatrefoil plan, with four conches round the main dome. Four massive fluted "elephant's foot" piers, 5 m (16 ft) in diameter, support not only the great wheel-like arches

Sultan Ahmet Mosque

bearing the main dome (height 43 m (141 ft), diameter 23·5 m (77 ft)) but also the arches of the lateral compartments, which take off at different heights. The four conches are flanked by smaller and shallower semi-domes. The monumental effect of the interior, which measures 51 by 53 m (167 by 174 ft), is reinforced by the different forms of the arches (the lower arches and the arches bearing the dome pointed, the smaller supporting arches round-headed).

Minarets

The Sultan Ahmet Mosque is the only one of Istanbul's mosques to have six minarets – four, each with three balconies, at the corners of the mosque and two smaller ones, with two balconies, at the north end of the forecourt.

Interior

The 260 windows, all of which once had stained glass, admit a flood of light. Only in the kıbla wall are there stained-glass windows (modern imitations) which give some impression of what the original windows were like.

Much of the walls and vaulting is covered with painted ornament, with blue the predominant colour, which is believed to have replaced earlier tile decoration. On the lower part of the walls, and particularly on the galleries and the Sultan's loge, there are 17th c. İznik tiles, some of them of exquisite quality, in floral and foliage designs (lilies, tulips, roses, vines, cypresses).

Other particularly notable features are the magnificent wooden ceiling, with floral and geometric ornament, under the Sultan's loge and the doors and shutters with their charming mother-of-pearl and ivory inlays.

141

Sultan Ahmet Camii

Interior

Stained-glass window

Subsidiary buildings

The mosque complex includes a number of subsidiary buildings, now put to a variety of uses: e.g. the former medrese at the north-west corner of the mosque precincts and the old Koranic school against the east side of the precinct wall.

Türbe of Sultan Ahmet I

In this large square türbe are the tombs of Sultan Ahmet I, his wife Kösem and three of his sons (Murat IV, Osman II and Prince Beyazit).

Pavilion of Ahmet I

At the south-east corner of the mosque precincts is a small pavilion (köşk) with direct access to the mosque. It has an interesting built-in mihrab.

Carpet Museum

This Pavilion of Ahmet I has housed since 1978 a Carpet Museum with a collection of valuable carpets, mainly Turkish. Items of particular interest:
carpets from Divriği (province of Sivas) and the Great Mosque at Milas (province of Muğla);
14th, 15th and 16th c. carpets with Kufic inscriptions round the edges;
carpets from Uşak (16th c.);
carpets from Bergama, Çanakkale, Gördes, Konya-Lâdik and Kula (16th and 18th c.);
17th c. carpets with fine figures of animals.

Woven Carpet Museum

Housed in some of the old craftsmen's shops on the south-east side of the mosque complex is a museum (opened 1981) of woven carpets (kilims, Kicim, Zili and Sumak carpets). Among the finest items in the collection are carpets and rugs of the 17th, 18th and 19th c. from Aydın, Adana, Gaziantep, Kayseri and Konya.

Sultan Ahmet III Çeşmesi

See Ahmet III Çeşmesi

*Sultan Mehmet Fâtih Külliyesi   C/D4/5
(Sultan Mehmet Fâtih Mosque Complex)

After the conquest of Constantinople in 1453 Sultan Mehmet Fâtih (the Conqueror) built a large mosque complex on the city's Fourth Hill, involving the destruction of the 4th c. Constantinian Church of the Holy Apostles. The first Fâtih Mosque, built in the 1460s, was designed by the architect Sinasettin Yusuf (Atik Sinan, Sinan the Elder). In 1509 and again in 1766 the mosque was badly damaged by earthquakes, and it was then replaced by a new Baroque building, completed in 1771; the architect was Mehmet Tahir Ağa.

Location
Fevzi Paşa Cad.

Bus stop
Fâtih

The mosque is square in plan. On each side of the central area with its mighty dome are smaller areas with semi-domes, while the four corner compartments are roofed with small domes. Two minarets, each with two balconies, flank the front of the mosque facing the forecourt. The interior, which is flooded with light, was renovated some years ago, when the repainting of the decoration followed earlier patterns brought to light during restoration; the new stained-glass windows similarly followed older models. The Baroque piers supporting the main dome are an interesting variant of the traditional "elephants' feet".

Mosque

The forecourt, like the mosque, is square and is surrounded by domed colonnades with columns of verd antique and pink granite. The octagonal ablution fountain in the centre of the court, shaded by tall vegetation, belonged to the original mosque.

Forecourt

In the cemetery behind the mosque is the türbe (rebuilt in the 18th c.) of the first Ottoman ruler of Istanbul. In its present form it is a two-storey Baroque structure on an octagonal plan.
Near by are the türbes of Fâtih's wife Gülbahar and Sultan Abdül Hamit I.

Türbe of Mehmet Fâtih

The Fâtih Mosque was originally surrounded by numerous associated buildings. The hospital, public kitchen and caravanserai have disappeared. The eight medreses – largely preserved – are regarded as the original nucleus of Istanbul University.
At the south-east corner of the mosque complex is a charming tabhane (hospice for travelling dervishes) which has recently been carefully restored and now houses an interesting collection of *objets d'art*.

Subsidiary buildings

*Sultan Selim I Camii (Sultan Selim Mosque)   C4/5

This mosque on the city's Fifth Hill was built by Süleyman the Magnificent in honour of his father. Designed by an architect from Tabriz, it was completed in 1522. The architecture is a

Location
Yavuz Selim Cad.

bus stop
Yavuz Selim

variant of the Bursa style. The main structure, square in plan, has a relatively flat dome which is borne on the four outer walls. This is flanked by two wings on a cross-in-square plan, each with nine small domes. At the junction between the mosque and the forecourt are two minarets with a single balcony.

Interior

The spacious interior (24·5 m (80 ft) square) is of imposing effect. Notable features of the decoration and furnishing are the İznik tiles (*cuerda seca* technique) of excellent quality and the fine marble mihrab and mimber.

Forecourt

The forecourt is surrounded by attractive domed colonnades with finely worked granite and marble columns. Other charming features are the octagonal marble fountain with a curved roof and the beautiful tiles above the windows.

Türbes

Outside the mosque (in front of the mihrab) is the Türbe of Sultan Selim I, with tile decoration of the finest quality. Near by are the türbe built by Sinan for four of Sultan Süleyman I's children and the Tomb of Sultan Abdül Mecit (d. 1861).

****Sultan Süleyman I Külliyesi** (Süleyman Mosque Complex)   D6

Location
Süleymaniye Cad.

The mosque complex built by Sultan Süleyman I, the Magnificent, on a platform high above the Golden Horn is one of the supreme achievements of Ottoman architecture. The mosque itself, built between 1550 and 1557, is a master work by the celebrated architect Sinan.

Bus stops
Beyazit, Üniverste

Outer court

The mosque stands on an area of ground levelled for the purpose and enclosed on three sides by a wall pierced with windows.

Forecourt

The forecourt has an air of dignity and solemnity, and has a massive three-storey gateway (fine stalactitic vaulting) on the west side. The clock-room (muvakkithane) in which the Mosque Astronomer worked was formerly attached to the gatehouse. The colonnades around the court have elegant porphyry, marble and granite columns. At the corners of the court are four minarets, two tall ones with three balconies and two shorter ones with two.
In the centre is a plain ablution fountain faced with light-coloured marble.

Mosque

The dimensions of the mosque, which was modelled on the Ayasofya (see entry), are overwhelming. This is true particularly of the central area, which measures 58·5 by 57·5 m (192 by 189 ft). Four massive piers support the main dome (height 47 m (154 ft), diameter 27·5 m (90 ft)), which is flanked on the east and west sides by semi-domes and borne on the north and south sides by arches supporting tympana pierced by windows. Between the main piers on the north and south sides are two 9 m (30 ft) high columns of granite or porphyry carrying the arches of the side aisles. The galleries, set back in the aisles, achieve considerable architectural effect.
The decoration of the interior creates an effect of grandeur. In the east wall, which has painted decoration, are marvellous stained-glass windows attributed to Şarhos İbrahim. On the

Mosque of Süleyman the Magnificent

Süleymaniye Camii

25 m
28 yd

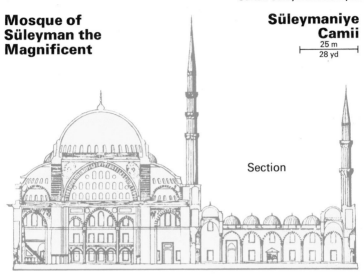

Section

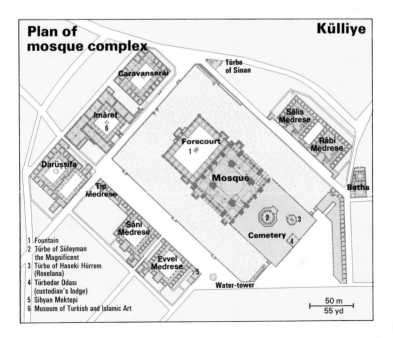

Plan of mosque complex

Külliye

Türbe of Sinan

Caravanserai

İmaret
6

Sâlis Medrese

Rabi Medrese

Darüşşifa

Forecourt
1

Mosque

Baths

Tıp Medrese

Sâni Medrese

2
3

Cemetery
4

1 Fountain
2 Türbe of Süleyman
   the Magnificent
3 Türbe of Haseki Hürrem
   (Roxelana)
4 Türbedar Odası
   (custodian's lodge)
5 Sibyan Mektepi
6 Museum of Turkish and Islamic Art

Evvel Medrese

5

Water-tower

50 m
55 yd

145

Süleyman Mosque

Süleyman Mosque: painted decoration

mihrab wall are beautiful İznik tiles (turquoise, deep blue and red on a white ground) in foliage and floral designs. The calligraphic inscriptions on plaques were the work of Ahmet Karahisarı and his pupil Hasan Çelebi. The main dome was painted in the 19th c. by the Fossati brothers, following models of the Ottoman Baroque period. At some points, remains of the original painting in blue and red have survived. In the current restoration work in the semi-domes the repainting is modelled on these remains of the original decoration. The mihrab and mimber are of Proconnesian marble. Note the fine woodwork, with ivory and mother-of-pearl inlays, of the Kuran kürsü, doors and shutters.

In the cemetery behind the mosque can be seen the octagonal Türbe of Süleyman the Magnificent, the largest tomb built by Sinan; it is surrounded by a columned portico.
The dome is double. The inner dome is painted in dark colours (wine-red, gold, dark brown) and spangled with fragments of precious stones, giving it the aspect of a starry sky. On the walls are beautiful İznik tiles.
In addition to Süleyman himself (sarcophagus in centre, with a white turban) his daughter Mihrimah and the later Sultans Süleyman II and Ahmet II are also buried here.
Türbe of Süleyman I

The Tomb of Haseki Hürrem (Roxelana), Süleyman the Magnificent's wife, is smaller and plainer, but the İznik tiles are finer than those in Süleyman's Türbe.
Türbe of Haseki Hürrem (Roxelana)

On the south-east side of the mosque complex is the Darül Hadis (Islamic school), consisting of a row of 22 cells with a pavilion-like superstructure.
Darül Hadis

The mosque bath-house diagonally across from the Islamic school is much in need of renovation.
Hamam

On the north side of the mosque precinct are the Salis Medrese (Third Medrese) and Rabi Medrese (Fourth Medrese), which together with two other medreses to the west formed an Islamic college.
Salis Medrese, Rabi Medrese

In a little garden at the north-east corner of the mosque precinct is the türbe which Sinan designed for himself, with a double canopy roof. On the south wall is an inscription by the poet Mustafa Sa'i, a friend of Sinan's.
Türbe of Sinan

These are the First and Second Medreses which formed part of the Islamic college. They now house the Süleyman Library, one of the leading institutions of its kind in Istanbul, with more than 32,000 manuscripts.
Evvel Medrese, Sâni Medrese

This medrese, adjoining the First and Second Medreses, was the medical school of the Ottoman Empire.
Tıp Medresesi

At the north-west corner of the mosque precinct is the former hospital, now converted to other purposes.
Darüssifa (Hospital)

See Türk ve Islâm Eserleri Müzesi (Museum of Turkish and Islamic Art)
Imâret (public kitchen)

Sultan Süleyman I Külliyesi

Main entrance of mosque

Tomb of a young woman

Türbe of Sinan

Minaret

Takkeci Camii (Takkeci Mosque, Hat-Maker's Mosque)   D2

The exterior of this mosque, built by the hat-maker Arakiyeci İbrahim Efendi in 1595, is not particularly impressive, but the interior is well worth a visit. The tile decoration, particularly on the mihrab wall and the window-framings, is among the finest in Istanbul. The wooden dome is painted in ray patterns.

Location
Near Topkapı

Bus stop
Topkapı

Taksim Meydanı (Taksim Square)   B8/9

Taksim Square is one of Istanbul's busiest traffic intersections. Some of the city's main traffic arteries radiate from the square, including Cumhuriyet Caddesi (see entry), which runs north, Gümüşsuyu Caddesi, which descends to Dolmabahçe Sarayı (see entry), Sıraselviler Caddesi, which leads to the harbour, and İstiklâl Caddesi (see entry), which runs south-west to Tünel Meydanı.
The square takes its name (taksim=division, distribution) from a cistern which distributed the water brought in from the Belgrade Forest (see Belgrat Ormanı) to the different parts of the city. It is now surrounded by numerous hotels, including two of Istanbul's new landmarks, the tower blocks of the Etap Marmara and the Hilton.

Location
Beyoğlu

Bus stop
Taksim

In the centre of the square is the Independence Monument, by the Italian sculptor Canonica (1928). It depicts Atatürk, the

Independence Monument

Independence Monument   *Traffic in Taksim Square*

149

"Father of Turkey", with General İsmet İnönü, Marshal Çakmak and other leaders of the fight for Turkish independence.

Atatürk Kültür Sarayı
(Opera House)

On the east side of the square stands the modern Atatürk Kültür Sarayı, the city's leading cultural centre, the scene of a variety of artistic events (opera, ballet, drama, concerts, etc.).
Opened in 1976, the new Opera House replaced the previous building, which was completed only in 1970 and soon afterwards burned down.

---

*Tekfur Sarayi (Imperial Palace)   B3

Location
Hoca Çakır Cad.

Bus stop
Edirnekapı

The Tekfur Palace, the Imperial residence in the later centuries of the Byzantine Empire, is now merely an imposing ruin. Built between the 11th and 14th c., it was probably part of the Blachernae complex. After the Fall of Constantinople, in a badly dilapidated state, it served for a time to house the Sultan's menagerie. In the 18th c. it became a porcelain manufactory, in the 19th a glass factory.

Architecture

The palace, of three storeys, is wedged in between the old Theodosian Walls and the Middle Byzantine outer wall. The main front facing the courtyard (opened up in 1955) is attractive, with its decorative pattern of alternating stone and brick. On the ground floor are two double arches supported on columns, on the first and second floors round-headed windows. The second floor has windows in all four walls, a

Tekfur Sarayı, the palace of the Byzantine Emperors

balcony on the east side and an apse-like projection on the south end.

To the north of the Tekfur Palace are scanty remains of the Byzantine Blachernae Palace, the origins of which go back to the time of the Emperor Anastasius (5th c.). The palace reached its greatest size and splendour in the time of the Comneni. Occupied for a time by the Latin Emperors, it was destroyed after the Ottoman conquest of Constantinople.

Blachernae Palace

*Tevfik Fikret Asiyani Müzesi (Tevfik Fikret Museum)

Idyllically situated on the Bosphorus is the house, built in 1906, of the poet Tevfik Fikret (d. 1915), one of the leading representatives of modern Turkish literature.

The house, named Asiyani, was opened to the public as a museum in 1945. It contains a variety of material on the poet's life and work, and shows the life-style enjoyed by well-to-do citizens of the Ottoman Empire in the early years of the 20th c.

Location
Near Rumeli Hisarı

Bus stop
Rumeli Hisarı

Boat landing-stage
Rumeli Hisarı

Theodosian Walls

See Land Walls

Tiled Pavilion

See Arkeoloji Müzesi, Çinili Köşk

*Tophane (Cannon Foundry)   C8

Istanbul's Tophane was the principal cannon foundry of the Ottoman Empire, already famous in the time of Mehmet the Conqueror. In the course of its history it underwent much alteration and rebuilding. In its present form it dates from 1803, in the reign of Sultan Selim III.

This large rectangular building, with its handsome brick and stone masonry, is given monumental effect by its eight great domes, borne on tall piers. Some years ago work began on the restoration of the building for use as offices, but this was not proceeded with. It is now occupied by the military and closed to the public.

Location
Defterdar Yokuşu

Bus stop
Tophane

This fountain, across the road from the Tophane, was erected in 1732, during the reign of Sultan Mahmut I. It is one of Istanbul's most beautiful fountains, with a large dome topped by attractive little lanterns.

Tophane Çeşmesi
(Tophane Fountain)

Topkapı Camii

See Ahmet Paşa Camii

Topkapı Sarayı or Eski Saray
(Cannon Gate Palace, Old Seraglio)

D8/9

Location
Seraglio Point

Bus stop
Sultanahmet

This palace of the Sultans, a city in itself, occupies the first of Constantinople's seven hills, the site of the acropolis and the original nucleus of the Greek town of Byzantion. The extensive complex of buildings, set in carefully tended gardens and surrounded by battlemented walls and towers, consists of an outer area, in which are Aya İrini Kilisesi, Arkeoloji (see entries) Müzesi and other buildings, and the Inner Seraglio. The first Ottoman building on the site was a summer palace built by Mehmet the Conqueror in 1468, which was enlarged by Süleyman the Magnificent to become his principal residence; and this remained the residence of the Sultans for centuries, until Abdül Mecit moved in 1855 to the Dolmabahçe Palace (see entry).

First Court

Bab-ı Hümayûn

The main gateway of the palace, Bab-ı Hümayûn (Imperial Gate), leads into the First Court, now used as a car park. It was once occupied by various buildings attached to the palace.

Bab-üs Selâm

The Bab-üs Selâm (Gate of Greetings), or Middle Gate, forms the entrance to the Inner Palace. Fronted by twin towers, it was huge wrought-iron gates (1525) from the workshop of Gayb bin Mehmet.
The left-hand tower was occasionally used as a prison for high dignitaries who had fallen into disfavour.

Sultan's throne, Topkapı Sarayı

**Topkapı Sarayı
(Cannon Gate Palace)**

Eski Sarayı
(Old Seraglio)

Bağdad Köşk

FOURTH

Sofa Köşk

Sünnet Odası

Revan Köşk

Mecidiye Köşk

COURT

Hırka-i Saadet

Clock Collection

Portraits and Miniatures

Calligraphy Collection

Offices

H a r e m
(see special plan)

THIRD

Ağalar Camii

Library of Ahmet III

COURT

Textile Collection

Arz Odası

Seferli Koğuşu

Kubbe Altı

Bab-üs Saadet

Arms and Armour

SECOND

COURT

Palace Kitchens

Beşir Ağa Camii

Bab-üs Selâm

FIRST

COURT

50 m
55 ft

Second Court

The Middle Gate leads into the Second Court, which measures 160 m (525 ft) by 130 m (425 ft). On the right are the old palace kitchens, on the left the Court Stables (exhibition of carriages and sedan-chairs), the Kubbe Altı, the Inner Treasury and the Harem (see p. 159).

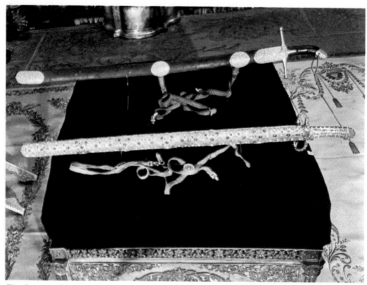

The Sword of the Prophet

Kitchens

The long frontage containing the palace kitchens was built in the time of Mehmet the Conqueror, and later restored by the famous architect Sinan. It is given its distinctive character by its 20 chimney-domes. Some 1200 cooks were employed in the kitchens, in which on days of high festival many thousands of meals had to be prepared.

The kitchens now house one of the world's largest collections of porcelain. Section 1: green celadon (Chinese dynasties of the 10th and 12th c.); blue-and-white ware of the Yüan dynasty (14th c.); Ming porcelain. Section 2: Ming blue-and-white ware. Sections 3 and 4: porcelain of the Ch'ing period (17th–20th c.); Japanese collection. Special collection: early Turkish plates and dishes.

Bab-üs Saadet

The Bab-üs Saadet (Gate of Felicity), also known as Ak Ağalar Kapısı (Gate of the White Eunuchs), gives access to the inner precincts of the palace. Important ceremonies took place in front of the gate, on the occasion of the enthronement of the Sultan, the distribution of bounties to the Janissaries, and so on.

Third Court (right-hand side)

Arz Odası

Beyond the Gate of Felicity is the Arz Odası (Audience Chamber), a richly appointed room in which the Padishah (Sultan), seated on his magnificent throne (cushions set with emeralds and pearls, elaborately ornamented wooden legs), received foreign envoys.

A diamond-encrusted Koran case

The east side of the Third Court is occupied by the Treasury range of buildings. The Seferli Koğuşu (Campaign Hall) houses a collection of splendid costumes worn by the Sultans, made of precious fabrics (brocade, taffeta, velvet, satin silk), together with costumes worn by the young Princes, specimens of material and prayer-rugs.

Seferli Koğusu

The old palace of Mehmet the Conqueror, later occupied by the Treasury, contains treasures of incalculable value.

Hazine-ı Hümayûn (Treasury)

Room 1:
Armour of Sultan Mustafa III, with gold plaques and settings of precious stones; Koran case encrusted with pearls; Sultan Murat IV's throne, with ivory and mother-of-pearl inlays; water jars, jugs and cups of the 16th and 17th c.; golden candelabra and water-pipes (nargilehs); jade vases; a walking-stick set with brilliants (presented to Sultan Abdül Hamit by the German Emperor William II); an Indian music-chest (17th c.); gold sorbet service, wash-basin and jug which belonged to Sultan Abdül Hamit; weapons encrusted with precious stones; a statuette decorated with pearls (presented to Sultan Abdül Aziz); gold plate.

Room 2:
Emerald prayer chains and quivers (16th c.); pendants of precious stones in gold settings, including superb examples which belonged to Sultans Abdül Hamit I and Ahmet I; plumes set with rubies and diamonds; the Topkapı Dagger, set with large emeralds and diamonds, on a pearl-encrusted gold

Baghdad Pavilion

cushion; Sultan Ahmet I's throne (walnut, with mother-of-pearl and tortoiseshell inlays); wood-carving; articles of rock-crystal and jade; a golden cradle for royal infants.

Spoonmaker's Diamond

Room 3:
Koran cases encrusted with precious stones; utensils of gold and enamel; a pendant which belonged to Sultan Mahmut II; the Kevkeb-ıDürri and Seb Cerag diamonds; incense-burners and rose-water sprinklers; the 86-carat Spoonmaker's diamond, set in silver and surrounded by 49 brilliants; diamond-studded gold chandeliers; various works of art, orders and medals; gold ceremonial throne (1558), measuring 1·08 by 1·78 m (3 ft 6 in by 5 ft 10 in) and weighing 250 kg (550 lb), plated with gold and set with precious stones; writing utensils.

Room 4:
Turkish-Indian throne, studded with pearls and emeralds (presented to Sultan Mahmut I by Shah Nadir of Persia); ivory dishes and other articles; reliquary of the Prophet's mantle; oil-lamps; spoons, prayer chains; weapons.

Gallery of Portraits and Miniatures

Calligraphic inscriptions, miniatures and other *objets d'art* of the Turkish and Islamic world (13th–17th c.); portraits of Ottoman rulers.

Clock Collection

Clocks of the 16th–20th c., including a clock in the form of a sphinx, encrusted with brilliants, presented to Sultan Abdül Mecit II by Tsar Nicholas II of Russia.

Here, in two vaulted rooms decorated with exquisite İznik tiles and fine woodwork, are displayed the relics and other sacred objects which Sultan Yavuz Selim brought back from his Egyptian campaign. Among them are the first Koran, written on gazelle-skin; relics of the Prophet Muhammad, in a special case (teeth, hair from his beard, earth from his tomb and a letter); and, in a room by themselves, the Prophet's mantle (Hırka-ı Saadet), standard and sword.

Pavilion of the Holy Mantle

This little pavilion, in which the Sultan's turbans were kept, was built in 1635. Octagonal in plan, it is decorated with tiles and marble, and has shutters inlaid with mother-of-pearl and tortoiseshell.

Rivan Köşkü
(Erevan Pavilion)

This little pavilion between the Rivan Köşkü and the Bağdad Köşkü, faced externally and internally with beautiful tiles, was used for the ceremonial circumcision of the sons of Sultans and viziers. Near by is a loggia in which the Sultans ate their evening meal during the Ramadan fast.

Sünnet Odası
(Circumcision Room)

The charm of the Baghdad Pavilion lies in its open colonnade (marble columns) and its tile decoration. From the dome hangs a gilded sphere.

Bağdad Köşkü
(Baghdad Pavilion)

Fourth Court

Just below the Erevan Pavilion is the Fourth Court.

The Mecidiye Pavilion (restaurant) was built in the 19th c., and is similar in style to Dolmabahçe Sarayı (see entry). From here there is a fine view over the Sea of Marmara.

Mecidiye Köşkü

The Sofa Pavilion, built in 1704, is one of Istanbul's oldest surviving timber buildings. The adjoining Hekimbaşı Tower was the domain of the Palace doctors.

Sofa Köşkü

Third Court (left-hand side)

On the south side of the Pavilion of the Holy Mantle is the manuscripts and calligraphy section, with a display of manuscripts, specimens of script, gold calligraphic inscriptions and books.

Calligraphy Section

This library, standing by itself, was built for Ahmet III in 1718. This domed and vaulted marble building, in the Tulip style, is decorated with İznik tiles of the highest quality. The sofas and bookshelves are masterpieces of craftsmanship.

Library of Sultan Ahmet III

The left-hand wing of Bab-üs Saadet contains a collection of textiles, including both hand-woven and machine-made materials, patterns for rugs and kilims, and figures from shadow-plays.

Textile Collection

Second Court (left-hand side)

At the north-west corner of the Second Court is the old Treasury, a 16th c. building with eight domes and underground

Collection of Arms and Armour

157

Bab-üs Selâm

Dining-Room of Ahmet III

A sumptuously decorated clock

Sultan's Bath, Harem

strongrooms. It now houses a collection of old and rare Turkish, Persian and Arabian arms and armour, including material of the Umayyad period (7th and 8th c.), armour or Mameluke times and military booty of the 15th–17th c.

Under the Baroque-style Tower of Justice (16th–19th c.; 41 m (135 ft high)) is the Kubbe Altı or Divan, built in the reign of Süleyman the Magnificent, with the council chamber in which the Sultan's Council of Viziers met. The Sultan was able to be present at the meetings of his Council, unobserved, behind a window grille in the Harem. The Grand Vizier also received foreign envoys in the Kubbe Altı.

Kubbe Altı

Harem

D8

Beyond the Tower of Justice is the Harem (from an Arabic word meaning "that which is forbidden"), a labyrinth of buildings erected at different times from the second half of the 16th c.

Under Islamic law the Sultan of the Ottoman Empire was permitted to have four principal wives. In addition he might have several favourite wives, who, like the principal wives, could wield great influence. There was no limit on the number of subsidiary wives the Sultan might have. The practice of segregating the ruler's wives and acknowledging his special position followed the example of Byzantine Court Customs, adapted to Islamic conditions.

Origins of the Harem

Hall of the Padishah, Harem

Harem
in Topkapı Sarayı

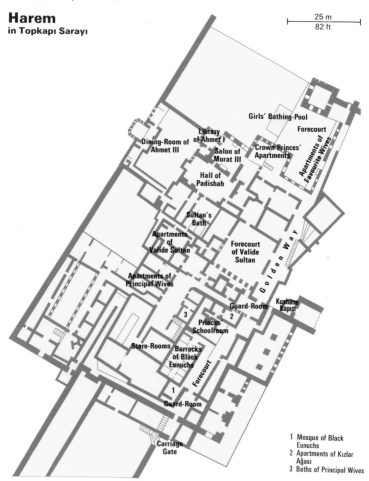

25 m
82 ft

Girls' Bathing-Pool

Forecourt

Library of Ahmet I

Dining-Room of Ahmet III

Salon of Murat III

Crown Princes' Apartments

Apartments of Favourite Wives

Hall of Padishah

Sultan's Bath

Apartments of Valide Sultan

Forecourt of Valide Sultan

Golden Way

Apartments of Principal Wives

Guard-Room

Kushane Kapısı

3

Princes' Schoolroom

2

Store-Rooms

Barracks of Black Eunuchs

1

Forecourt

Guard-Room

Carriage Gate

1 Mosque of Black Eunuchs
2 Apartments of Kızlar Ağası
3 Baths of Principal Wives

Tour of the Harem

The Harem is entered by the Carriage Gate beyond the Kubbe Altı, which leads into the Guard-Room of the White Eunuchs, with a decoration of Kütahya tiles. A small door on the left opens into the Mosque of the Black Eunuchs, which has walls faced with tiles right up to the ceiling and a fine mimber with mother-of-pearl inlays. A paved and vaulted passage gives access to the Barracks of the Black Eunuchs, a long dark corridor flanked by three floors of small rooms. Beyond this are the apartments of the Kızlar Ağası (The "Aga in charge of the girls") and the Schoolroom of the Princes.

160

Apartments of the Principal Wives:
In the entrance hall (fine Kütahya tiles) is a wooden chest of
notable quality. The principal apartment has tile decoration and
beautiful stained-glass windows (restored).

Apartments of the Valide Sultan (Sultana Mother):
The rooms are sumptuously decorated: coffered ceilings with
gilt ornament; windowless walls, with 18th c. landscape-
paintings; Chinese vases in windows. In the bedroom the bed,
with rich gilt ornament, stands on a dais. Adjoining the
bedroom is the prayer-room.

Sultan's Bath:
This is the finest bathroom in the Harem, consisting of a rest-
room, a massage-room, a dressing-room and the bath itself, of
white marble, with a grille to protect the Sultan from attempts
on his life while he was having his bath.

Hall of the Padishah:
This vaulted hall, probably designed by Sinan, was remodelled
in Rococco style in the reign of Sultan Osman III. The music
gallery, the silk-upholstered benches, the fountain, the crystal
mirrors, the splendid chandeliers and the sumptuous tile
decoration all bear witness to the importance of this room as a
banqueting hall and the setting for celebrations and entertainments. On either side of the Sultan's throne are magnificent
Chinese vases. A secret door in a mirror-fronted cabinet
enabled the Sultan to make his way to other parts of the
building if he wished.

Salon of Murat III:
This is one of the finest rooms in the Harem: domed, with blue
and coral-red tile decoration and fine chimneypieces with
copper hoods (16th c.). The plashing of the water in the
fountain was designed to prevent conversations from being
overheard.

Library of Ahmet I:
This is a charming little room, with exquisite tile decoration, a
valuable cabinet inlaid with mother-of-pearl and windows
framed in mother-of-pearl.

Dining-Room of Ahmet III (Fruit Room):
The walls and ceiling are decorated with charming paintings of
fruit and flowers. Fine circular metal table (sini).

Crown Princes' Apartments:
These rooms are lavishly decorated with marble, gilt ornament,
tiles and stained glass. Beyond this are the rooms of the
gözdeler (favourite wives) and hasekiler (wives who had borne
the Sultan a son).

Golden Way:
This dark corridor 46 m (150 ft) long was the scene of notable
events. Here the cariyeler (young girls destined for the Sultan's
pleasure) passed their leisure time, and here one of them fought
off the conspirators who were trying to kill the future Mahmut
II. On days of festival the Sultans caused gold coins to be
scattered here.

Kuşhane Kapısı (Birdcage Gate):
Through this gate, where the tour ends, food used to be
brought into the Harem.

Town Hall

See Belediye Sarayı

Troy (Hisarlık; Turuva, Truva, Trova; Gk Ilion or Ilios; Lat. Ilium Novum)

Location
260 km (160 miles) SW of
Istanbul as the crow flies

Access
By road, car or bus from
Istanbul via Tekirdağ and
Çanakkale (Dardanelles ferry
from Eceabat; 380 km (236
miles)), or via Bursa,
Bandırma and Çanakkale
(580 km (360 miles)); by
boat, regular service from
Istanbul to Çanakkale, then
bus

Troy, the excavated site of the chief town of the ancient Troad, made famous by Homer's "Iliad", lies on a hill now some 40 m (130 ft) high a little to the south of the junction of the Dardanelles with the Aegean. The hill is a wedge-shaped outlier of an area of higher ground which broadens out towards the east, rising steeply to the alluvial plain of the Küçük Menderes (the Scamander of the Greeks) and the Dümrek Çayı (the ancient Simois).

The hill rising out of the surrounding plain offered a good strategic site for a fortress, far enough away from the sea to be safe from surprise attacks but near enough to be able to keep a watch on the entrance to the Dardanelles. No doubt only the acropolis was on the hill, with the rest of the town extending over the river plain. This situation enabled the town to achieve early prosperity, but also exposed it to repeated attacks and frequent destruction. In consequence there are no buildings left standing on the site: all that the visitor will see are the excavators' trenches and the various settlement levels they have brought to light – though what he does see is extraordinarily impressive, both as a revelation of a history going back 5000 years and as a demonstration of what archaeology can achieve in unravelling the distant past.

Troy I
(3000–2500 B.C.)

The culture of the lowest occupation levels on the Hill of Kumtepe, 5 km (3 miles) north-west of Troy, is older than that of Troy I. Excavation has shown that there was a settlement on the rocky hill of Hisarlık some 5000 years ago.

Troy II
(2500–2300 B.C.)

About the middle of the 3rd millennium the Troy I settlement was extended towards the south. With an area of 8000 sq. m (9500 sq. yd), it may have had a population of some 3000. The fortifications of this Troy II settlement were much more extensive and more massive than those of Troy I, being built of large irregularly shaped (Cyclopean) blocks, topped by a brick superstructure reinforced by timber beams. In the centre of the circuit of walls stood the palace of the ruler. The houses were now more spacious and more numerous, with stone foundations. It was in this level that Heinrich Schliemann found what he called the Treasure of Priam (gold and silver vessels, gold jewellery, etc.).

About 2300 B.C. Troy II was destroyed by fire. Schliemann was convinced until shortly before his death that this was Homer's Troy.

Troy III
(2300–2200 B.C.)

The fire which destroyed Troy II left a 2 m (6 ft) thick layer of rubble and ashes. Later settlers lived in primitive huts and lived by hunting. This settlement, too, was destroyed in circumstances that are not understood.

Troy IV
(2200–2100 B.C.)

A new walled settlement grew up on the ruins of Troy III.

Troy V
(2100–1900 B.C.)

This, too, was a rather meagre little settlement, defended only by a weak circuit of walls. The rather more numerous artefacts found in this level, however, point to the introduction of a new culture from the Aegean (Mycenaean influence).

Troy VI
(1900–1240 B.C.)

The new town now built, the Cyclopean walls of which are the most striking features of the site, enjoyed its period of greatest prosperity between the 16th and 13th c. The upper town, covering an area 200 m (220 yd) by 300 m (330 yd), was surrounded by a 10 m (33 ft) high wall, rising in four terraces. No trace has yet been found of a lower town. The cemetery in which the remains of the dead were deposited, after cremation, in pottery urns, lay 500 m (550 yd) to the south.

Troy VIIa
(c. 1230 B.C.)

After what is believed to have been destruction by earthquake about 1240 B.C. the town seems to have been rebuilt. The population's way of life remained unchanged. A century later, however, the town was again destroyed.

Troy VIIb
(1220–1070 B.C.)

After the destruction of Troy VIIa the site was occupied by Illyrians. Perhaps the last incomers were the Dardanians, who gave their name to the Dardanelles.

Troy VIII
(1070–350 B.C.)

In the 8th c. the Illyrian settlement became a Greek colony. In 652 the Cimmerians, after defeating King Gyges of Lydia, moved into the Troad, without displacing the Greeks. In 547 King Cyrus of Persia incorporated Troy in the Persian satrapy (governorship) of Phrygia.

Excavations, Troy

Troy

In 334 B.C. Alexander the Great crossed the Dardanelles and took Troy, where he offered a sacrifice to Athena Ilias. About 300 Lysimachus built a harbour for the town at the mouth of the Scamander and replaced the old Temple of Athena by a splendid new one in marble.

Between 278 and 270 the town was held by the Galatians, a Celtic people. Thereafter, until 190 B.C., it changed hands several times. Whereas the importance of Troy had hitherto depended on its Temple of Athena, which was ranked equal in status with the Temple of Artemis at Ephesus, it now enjoyed Roman favour as the city of Aeneas, Rome seeing itself as the political heir of Troy.

Until the incursion of the Goths about A.D. 262 Troy had a period of high prosperity, which continued into Early Byzantine times: indeed, Constantine the Great even contemplated making Troy his capital. With the recognition of Christianity as the State religion, however, the old temples fell into ruin, and Troy's glory rapidly faded. In 394 the Olympic Games were forbidden, and a lime-kiln was built in the theatre in which the stones of the Temple of Athena were burned.

In the Middle Ages Troy still had a fortress, and until the 13th c. it was the see of a bishop, but after its conquest by the Ottomans in 1306 the town rapidly fell into ruin. The remains were used by the Turks as a quarry of building stone for their mosques and tombs. Grass grew over the site, and Troy fell into oblivion.

The rediscovery of Troy

The first Westerner to visit Troy seems to have been a French traveller named Pierre Belon (before 1553). In 1610 the English poet George Sandys looked for the ruins of Troy on the hill of Hisarlık. Between 1781 and 1791 the Comte de Choiseul-Gouffier and a French archaeologist named Lechevalier explored the Troad and localised Homer's Troy on the hill of Balıdağ, near Bunarbaşı, 8 km (5 miles) south-east of Hisarlık. Helmuth von Moltke, then a Captain on the Prussian General Staff, also saw Bunarbaşı as the site of Troy.

From 1859 onwards Frank Calvert, an Englishman who owned part of the hill of Hisarlık, carried out excavations there. In 1868 Heinrich Schliemann (1822–90), a German businessman who had made a large fortune in St Petersburg, came to the Troad to look for Troy; after a brief exploratory excavation on Burnabaşı, which yielded only a thin layer of rubble, he turned his attention to Hisarlık. Thereafter, in a series of excavation campaigns between 1870 and 1890, he was able to prove the correctness of his choice and to defend his case against the passionately held views of other archaeologists. Until 1882, it is true, his excavations showed little concern with exact observation or the conservation of the remains, and much evidence was destroyed for ever, particularly as a result of the broad trench which he drove across the site from north to south; but thereafter, with the collaboration of the German archaeologist Wilhelm Dörpfeld (1853–1940), the work was carried on more scientifically. Unfortunately Schliemann himself did not live to see the final result of his excavations. After discovering, on 14 June 1873, the so-called "Treasure of Priam" (which was shipped to Germany in dramatic circumstances and then lost during the Second World War), he held Troy II to be the city of Priam. It was only his 1890 excavations and Dörpfeld's excavations of 1893–94 (after Schliemann's death) that suggested that Troy VI should be assigned to the Mycenaean period. The excavations were continued in 1932–38 by Carl W. Blegen of Cincinnati University.

Since the story of the Trojan Horse which led to the Fall of Troy was associated with the earthquake god Poseidon, scholars such as Schachermeyr identify Troy VI, which was destroyed in an earthquake, with Homer's Troy; others would see Troy VIIa as the city of Priam.

At the end of the approach road to the site (car park), near the East Gate, is a small museum with finds from the site and illustrations of the different settlements.

Museum

Just to the right of Theatre C is the South Tower (G9, VIi on plan) of the Mycenaean settlement (Troy VI), which is crossed by a marble-faced Roman wall. The paved roadway (G9, VIT) to the right of the tower is 3·3 m (10 ft) wide. The East Wall, to the right, had a massive substructure some 6 m (20 ft) high and 5 m (16½ ft) thick, with a distinct batter (slope), which was visible from the exterior. On top of this, from 1 m (40 in) above the ground level of the settlement, was a vertical superstructure of flat, square, almost regularly dressed stones.

South Tower

East Wall

Some 9 m (30 ft) east of the South Gate is one of the characteristic features of this wall, a vertical offset of 10–15 cm (4–6 in), recurring every 9–10 m (33 ft).

The first of these offsets is within the Roman theatre (Theatre B; H/I 8/9 on plan), built over the wall. The lowest row of seating is of marble.

Theatre B

Beyond Theatre B the wall continues north-east. Cutting across a long Roman wall of regularly dressed stone, it comes to the South-East Tower (I/K 7/8, VIh on plan), which was originally two-storeyed.

South-East Tower

To the left (west) of the South-East Tower, separated from the wall by the breadth of a street, are houses of the Mycenaean settlement: first in area VIG (H 7/9 on plan), which is cut by a thick Roman wall of dressed stone (the south wall of the stylobate of the temple precinct), then in area VIF (H/I 6/7 on plan) to the north, farther from the walls, and, still farther north, in areas VI E and VI C (H/I 5/6). The houses of Troy VI lay on a number of concentric terraces round the hill (see section on plan). The King's Palace no doubt stood on the highest point. Building VI F (H/I 7) was a hall measuring 12 by 8·40 m (39 by 28 ft), with two doors but no vestibule. House VI E is particularly well built, with an east wall of carefully coursed stone set deep into the ground. To the right (east) of VI F and VI E are rooms (K 5–7, VII) with storage jars (pithoi) set into the ground; they belong to Troy VII and are built over a Troy VI street. Adjoining VI F was a deep rock-cut well. Abutting on the west side of VI E is the rear wall of building VI G on the second terrace, the front part of which can be seen on the far side of the trench. Built into the front part is the stone base of a timber column.

Mycenaean houses

To the north of VI E, on the right, is the East Gate (K 6, VI S), on one of the radial ramps which lead up to the town. After passing through a breach in the Roman wall of dressed stone which bore the columns at the east end of the temple, we come to a projecting wall coming from the north, which together with a

East Gate

wall from the south forms a curving passage some 10 m (33 ft) long leading to the East Gate (1·80 m (6 ft) wide).

North-East Gate

Continuing north round the outside of the outer wall, we come to the massive North-East Gate (K 4, VIg) in the Mycenaean walls. The 6 m (20 ft) high substructure of fine dressed stone, with a distinct batter, once bore a superstructure of brick, giving the gate a commanding height. Within the gate is a square rock-cut well going down to a considerable depth (B b on plan), which long remained in use. In the Troy VIII period a flight of steps was constructed on the north side of the tower, leading down to another well outside the tower. The great retaining wall to the south-east dates from the Roman period.

Climbing up beyond the tower, continuing straight ahead from the main staircase and turning left at the end of a stone-flagged corridor, we come to another well (B a on plan), which, like the one in the North-East Gate, is cut through the rock to reach water (which still collects in the well).

Temple of Athena

Above the wall at this point is a level area once occupied by Troy's famous Temple of Athena. The magnificent new temple, which had been promised by Alexander the Great, was built by Lysimachus, but of this little survives. The columns, metopes (Helios on his four-horse chariot) and other marble fragments to be seen here probably belong for the most part to the temple built by Augustus and later several times restored. Its ground-plan (35·20 m (115 ft) by 16·40 m (54 ft)) can be identified from the deep trenches in which its foundations were laid on a basis of sand, rammed hard. On the far side of the paved corridor are the foundations of the altar (I/K 4, IX Z). In the centre of the wall of the southern precinct of the temple, facing the main gateway into the acropolis, was a gate with four columns along the front (G 7, IX D).

West Wall

Some 70 yards from Theatre C (E/F 9/10 on plan) we come to a large building of the Mycenaean period (C 7/8, VI M) on a 4 m (13 ft) high terrace which, on the basis of the large storage jars (pithoi) and other objects found in the third room, is known

Kitchen Building

as the Kitchen Building. A flight of steps behind this building, to the north, led up to the second terrace (VI N).

Some 25 yards beyond this the broad ring wall comes to an end. After a gap of some 7 yards, marking the position of an earlier west gate, it is continued by a narrower wall of excellent stone masonry. Almost up against this wall is a large and well-built house (A/B 6, VI A) consisting of a main hall preceded by a vestibule. Opposite the north corner of this house are the remains of a still larger house of the same type (VI B).

Here the Mycenaean wall, which enclosed the whole of the acropolis in a circuit of some 540 m (590 yd), two-thirds of which are preserved, comes to an end; part of the west side and the whole of the north side have been destroyed.

To the east of houses VI A and B, below, can be seen a ramp leading up to gate FM (C 6 on plan) from a lower circuit of walls revealed by excavation and continuing up the hill; the easiest access to it is from the south. This was a side entrance to the

Prehistoric fort

prehistoric fort (Troy II), the mud-brick stronghold destroyed by fire which Schliemann at first took for the citadel of Priam. It has a circumference of some 300 m (300 yd), now almost completely exposed. It can be seen in the banks of earth that have been left standing (E 4/5, E 6 and F 4/5 on plan) as a layer,

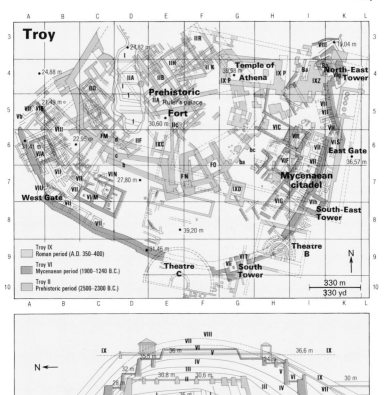

between 1 and 2 m (40 and 80 in) thick, of yellow, red or black rubble from the fire.

On either side of the ramp extends the ring wall of the fort, which had a substructure of limestone blocks, showing little sign of dressing, between 1 and 8 m (3 and 25 ft) in height. Higher up the ramp is a gate (C 6, FM on plan). To the right can be seen three different lines of wall (b, c, d). The gate farther to the right (east), FN (E/F 6/7), was the main entrance in the earlier period. Beyond this again is another gate (FO), the main entrance in the later phase of Troy II, which is broadly similar to gate FM.

Ring wall

167

Some 15 yards north-west of gate FO, on the far side of a courtyard which was once covered with pebbles, is a small propylaion (E 5/6, IIC). Its massive sill-stone, 3 m (10 ft) long and 1·10 m (43 in) wide, is still *in situ*.

**Megaron
(Palace)**

The propylaion is the entrance to a complex of buildings in the centre of the Troy II citadel which was evidently the residence of the ruler of the city. Off a gravelled court opened the dwellings of the ruler and his wife, children and relatives. The main building, directly opposite the propylaion, is the Megaron (D/E 4/5, IIA) or Great Hall, preceded by a portico. In the centre of the hall was a fireplace. The walls, the structure of which can be seen very clearly here, are 1·44 m (4 ft 9 in.) thick; the height of the building is unknown. No doubt it had a flat roof of clay and reeds with an opening over the hearth. To the right was a smaller building with a portico, a main hall, a rear chamber and a small portico at the back. On either side of the courtyard were other buildings of similar type.

Returning to the gate (FM) on the ramp, we find beyond it a similar group of smaller houses (C 4/5 on plan). There was probably another group in the northern part of the citadel, now destroyed.

"Treasure of Priam"

Some 6 m (20 ft) north-west of the ramp Schliemann found the so-called "Treasure of Priam", built into a cavity in the brick superstructure of the ring wall. (It later found its way to the Museum of Prehistory in Berlin,. but disappeared during the Second World War.) Similar finds of jewellery and precious vessels, weapons and implements made of gold, silver, electron (an alloy of gold and silver) and bronze have been made elsewhere in the Troy II level (Late Chalcolithic period).

In the great north—south trench (D 2-5 on plan) which Schliemann drove across the site, and which passes between the first and second groups of Troy II houses, some house walls of small stones bound with earth-mortar belonging to the two ancient settlements of Troy I have been preserved.

The remains of Troy III, IV, VII and VIII have little to interest the ordinary visitor. To the left of the gate on the ramp are house walls, partly built of undressed stone, which Schliemann took for the Palace of Priam but which are in fact houses of Troy III. Of Troy IV there are only scanty remains.

Troy V was surrounded by a wall only 1–1·30 m (40–50 in.) thick, which was gradually replaced in Troy VI by a new and better wall.

Of Troy VII there survive some remains of walls, mainly between the citadel wall of Troy VI and the first terrace walls. They belong to two quite different periods. First the walls and gates of Troy VI were repaired by a simple rural people, still using Mycenaean pottery, who built their houses, similar in plan to those of Troy VI, against the inner side of the walls. Remains of these houses can be seen on either side of gate VI S (J/K 5–7, VII on plan), with numerous large storage jars, and at the West Gate (VI U; also remains of a second inner circle of houses). At the same spots are other walls of a different kind, distinguished by the large irregular stones set on end (orthostats) over the foundations, which belonged to larger houses.

The evidence from Troy VIII shows that in that period Aeolian Greeks established a fortified settlement, restoring the old Troy VI walls by patching them with small stones. As a result of the Roman replanning of the town very little survives from this phase.

The area of the lower town on the plateau to the south and east of the hill has not so far been very much explored. In the earlier periods there seems to have been little settlement here, and it was not until the Hellenistic period that a small township grew up, to become in Roman times the town whose enclosing wall, 3500 m (3800 yd) long and 2·50 m (8 ft) thick, can still be traced. To this period also belongs the theatre at the north-east corner of the site. In test digs to the south of Theatres B and C the walls and granite columns of a stoa were discovered. The agora (market-place) is believed to have been in this area.

Lower town

Tulip Mosque

See Lâleli Camii

Tünel (Tunnel; underground funicular)   C7

The Tunnel, the subterranean funicular from the foot of the Galata Hill to the south end of İstiklâl Caddesi, 58 m (190 ft) higher up, can claim to be one of the world's oldest underground railways. Built by French engineers, it was opened in 1875.

Two cars joined by a cable run a shuttle service on the 614 m (672 yd) long track, which has a maximum gradient of 26 per cent.

Route
Tersane Cad.,
Karaköy–Tünel, Şişhane

The Tunnel, Istanbul's underground funicular

Türbe of Sinan

See Sultan Süleyman I Külliye

*Türk ve İslâm Eserleri Müzesi   D6
(Museum of Turkish and Islamic Art)

Location
Şifahane Sok.

Bus stops
Beyazit, Atatürk Bulvarı

Opening times
Tues.–Sun. 9 a.m.–5 p.m.

Admission charge

Charge for photography

The Museum of Turkish and Islamic Art is housed in the former public kitchen (Imâret) and the Sultan Süleyman I Külliye (see entry). In the colonnades and in five other rooms are displayed a variety of works of art of the highest quality.

Ceramics:
Samarra ware (the oldest Turkish glazed ware), Rakka ware (12th c.), Keşan ware, Anatolian tiles (13th c.), ceramics and tiles of various periods (particularly the Early Ottoman period).

Carpets:
Carpets from the Alaadin Mosque in Konya (13th c.); carpets from Uşak and Bergama (16th–18th c.); prayer-rugs from Gördes, Kula, Konya and Lâdik; carpets from the Caucasus and Persia; Anatolian kilims.

Metalwork:
Articles in gold, silver, copper and bronze, including candlesticks, rose-water flasks, caskets, etc., of the Seljuk, Mameluke and various Ottoman periods.

Manuscripts:
Early copies of the Koran (in Kufic script on gazelle-skin), Turkish and Persian miniatures (15th–18th c.), Turkish calligraphy (15th–19th c.).

Uludağ

See Bursa

*Üniversite (University)   D5/6

Location
Üniversite Cad., Ordu Cad., Takvimhane Cad.

Bus stop
Beyazit Meydanı

Istanbul University (c. 30,000 students in 1983), founded by Sultan Abdül Mecit in 1845, occupies the site of Mehmet the Conqueror's palace, the Eski Saray (Old Palace). In the gardens of the University is a prominent landmark, the Beyazit Tower. From Beyazit Square an imposing gate in Oriental style leads into the courtyard and gardens in which are the main University building and the Beyazit Tower. The main building, constructed in the 19th c. to the design of the French architect Auguste Bourgeois, is in the Historical style, imitating the architecture of the past. It originally housed the Sultan's Ministry of War (Seraskerat).
In the 1930s the building was altered and enlarged to accommodate the University's central services, including the University administration.

Gateway of the University

To the west of Beyazit Square are the new University buildings erected in the 1950s, with monumental doorways and huge columned halls. The architecture betrays the influence of the Stuttgart architect Paul Bonatz, who was a professor at the Istanbul College of Technology from 1946 to 1954.

Beyond the University gateway is the 50 m (165 ft) high Beyazit Tower, built in 1928 to replace an old timber fire-watcher's tower. From its viewing-platform (180 steps) there is a magnificent panoramic view of the city (see cover picture). The tower also serves as a weather-forecasting station.

Blue signal: fair
Green signal: rain
Yellow signal: mist or fog
Red signal: snow

Beyazit Tower

Üsküdar (Scutari)   C/D11/12

In spite of its rapid growth in size and population and the effects of modern road development, Istanbul's Asiatic suburb of Üsküdar (traditionally known as Scutari) has managed to preserve its Oriental character, at least in the old core of the town. One of the first Greek colonies on the Bosphorus was established here under the name of Chrysopolis, and, thanks to its situation, the town soon became a considerable centre of trade. Until the 19th c., it was the terminus of a caravan route along which the treasures of the East were transported to Europe.

Location
Asiatic side of Bosphorus

Bus stop
Üsküdar

Boat landing-stage
Üsküdar

The mosques of Üsküdar

Ayazma Camii (Ayazma Mosque)   C11

Location
Selâmsiz

The Ayazma Mosque, situated on a hill, is a Baroque building erected by Sultan Mustafa III in 1760–61 in the gardens of the old Ayazma Palace.

The mosque is built on a rectangular plan, measuring 14 by 18 m (46 by 59 ft). The main dome rests on a drum pierced by windows, which in turn is borne on "elephants' feet". The tiers of windows admit a flood of light which illuminates the beautiful marble-work on the windows, the columns of the gallery and the mihrab, mimber and Kuran kürsü. In addition to the pavilions and the fountain in the forecourt the mosque complex includes a primary school and a hamam (unfortunately much dilapidated).

Eski Valide Sultan Camii (Old Mosque of the Valide Sultan)   C12

Location
Valide Imâret Sok.

The Old Valide Sultan Mosque, also known as the Atik Valide Mosque, was built in 1583 by Nûrbânu Sultan, wife of Sultan Selim II and mother of Murat III. It is a late work by the great architect Sinan.

Originally the mosque had only a single dome (diameter 13 m (43 ft)), borne on six arches which also carried semi-domes; the side domes were added later. The mosque is flanked by two minarets with a single balcony.

The finest features in the interior are the tiles on the mihrab, which date from the 16th c., and the woodwork, particularly that of the windows, inlaid with mother-of-pearl.

In the forecourt is an ablution fountain with an openwork marble screen, which is one of the finest of its kind.
Below the mosque is a medrese, to the east of it the old hospital, to the west the caravanserai and the public kitchen – two institutions which were extremely popular in the 17th c. Still farther east is a bath-house (hamam).

İskele Camii (İskele Mosque)   C12

The İskele Mosque, at the Üsküdar landing-stage (iskele) on the Asiatic shore of the Bosphorus, was built by Sinan in 1547 for Mihrimah Sultan, daughter of Süleyman I and wife of his Grand Vizier, Rüstem Paşa.

Location
Near Üsküdar Iskelesi

The main dome rests on a drum with 16 windows, which in turn is borne on four columns. The three semi-domes round the dome are each flanked by two smaller semi-domes, giving the structure a very distinctive character. Unusual, too, are the round windows, here used by Sinan for the first time.
The mihrab and mimber are of finely worked marble. The window-frames, doors (of ebony) and the Kuran kürsü are notable for the beauty of their ivory and mother-of-pearl inlays. The inner vestibule, facing the Bosphorus, has five domes. The outer vestibule, in the form of a gallery, is particularly charming. In front of the mosque, on the landing-stage, is a beautiful marble fountain erected in the reign of Sultan Ahmet III.
The mosque complex also includes a medrese, a primary school (now a children's library), a bath-house, a public kitchen and a guest-house.

*Karacaahmet Mezarliği (Cemetery)   D/E12

Above Üsküdar is one of the largest cemeteries in the East, its old trees (mainly cypresses) giving it the air of a park. It contains large numbers of finely carved and decorated tombstones, mostly in marble. On the north side of the cemetery is an old Convent of the Howling Dervishes.

Location
1·5 km (1 mile) SE of centre of Üsküdar

Rum Mehmet Paşa Camii (Rum Mehmet Paşa Mosque)   C12

The Rum Mehmet Paşa Mosque, built in the 15th c. by Mehmet the Conqueror's Greek Grand Vizier, Mehmet Paşa, is commandingly situated on the Hill of Semsipaşa. With its T-shaped ground-plan (square central dome with a semi-dome to the rear, two small domed rooms on either side) it is typical of the Early Ottoman mosques of the Bursa type. It shows Byzantine influence.

Location
Semsipaşa Cad., Üsküdar

The main dome (diameter 11 m (36 ft)) is borne on a drum with eight windows. The large arches are built of brick. The vestibule is roofed by five small domes.
Near the south corner of the mihrab with its semi-dome is the octagonal türbe of the founder.

Yeni Valide Camii (New Valide Mosque)   C12

The classical-style New Valide Mosque was built in 1710, probably by Gülnaş Emetullah, wife of Sultan Mehmet IV and mother of Mustafa II and Ahmet III.

Location
Üsküdar Meydanı

The main dome, like that of the Rüstem Paşa Camii (see entry), is borne on eight piers. Around it, at the corners of the square prayer-hall, are four semi-domes. There are two charming minarets, each with two balconies.

The mihrab and mimber are finely worked. Round the mihrab are very beautiful Kütahya tiles. The galleries, roofed by small domes, have marble screens. The walls are also faced with marble.

The south doorway is notable for its marble decoration. In the centre of the forecourt is an octagonal ablution fountain with a domed roof.

The mosque complex also includes the open türbe of the foundress, a drinking-fountain and, farther away, a public kitchen.

Vakıfhan   D7

Location
Hamidiye Cad., Sirkeci

Bus stops
Sirkeci, Eminönü

The Vakıfhan office block, begun in 1914, is of considerable architectural interest. It is one of the most important buildings of the Turkish architect Kemalettin, successfully combining the Historical style with an enthusiasm for modern technology (e.g. lifts in special domed shafts) which was germinating in the early 20th c.

Valens, Aqueduct of

See Bozdoğan Kemeri

Valide Camii (Valide Mosque)   D5

Location
Corner of Atatürk Bulvarı
and Ordu Cad., Aksaray

Bus stop
Aksaray

The Valide Mosque was built by Pertevniyal Sultan, wife of Sultan Mahmut II and mother (valide) of Sultan Abdül Aziz. It is not certain whether the mosque was designed by the celebrated Balyan family of architects or the Italian architect Montani.

Set in a large garden court, the mosque is in classical style, on a square plan. The main dome rests on an unusually high drum pierced by windows. The monumental gateway of the courtyard is flanked by beautiful fountains.

Walls

See Land Walls, Sea Walls

*Yalova

Location
45 km (28 miles) SE of
Istanbul as the crow flies

The little port of Yalova (alt. 0–130 m (0–425 ft); pop. 25,000), in the province of Istanbul, is beautifully situated on the south side of İzmit Bay. The ferries from Istanbul and Kartal to Yalova considerably shorten the distance to Bursa.

Yalova Kaplıcaları (Baths of Yalova)

A few kilometres south-west of the town are thermal springs
(chalybeate, carbonated, sulphurous, radioactive) which have
been known since ancient times (featuring in the tale of the
Argonauts as Pythia). They were much frequented in Greek and
Roman times, and among those who came here to seek a cure
in later times were the Byzantine Emperor Constantine the
Great, the Empress Theodora, Ottoman potentates and Atatürk,
who visited the spa frequently (Atatürk House). Treatment at
Yalova is recommended for a wide range of complaints, from
kidney and bladder conditions to rheumatic diseases and
nervous disorders. The facilities at Yalova spa are being
brought up to the most modern standards (new hotels and
treatment establishments), and it is now one of the most
esteemed spas in western Asia.

---

*Yedikule (Castle of Seven Towers)   F1

The Fortress of Yedikule grew out of the Golden Gate in the
Theodosian land walls (see entry). The Golden Gate, a
triumphal arch erected by the Byzantine Emperor Theodosius I,
was enlarged by Theodosius II, who added four towers. After
the Conquest of Constantinople by Mehmet Fâtih three further,
less massive, towers were built. Under the Ottoman Sultans
Yedikule was used as an arsenal and treasury and later also as
a prison. In 1474 the Grand Vizier, Mahmut Paşa, was
imprisoned here, and here in 1622 Sultan Osman II and Davut
Paşa were murdered. Thoroughly restored in recent years,
Yedikule is now a museum.

The central feature of the castle is the Golden Gate, so called
because it originally had gilded doors. It is now flanked by fine
marble pylons. The hexagonal plan of the fortress shows the
influence of Renaissance military architecture in Europe.

Location
Yedikule Cad.

Suburban railway station
Yedikule

Bus stop
Yedikule

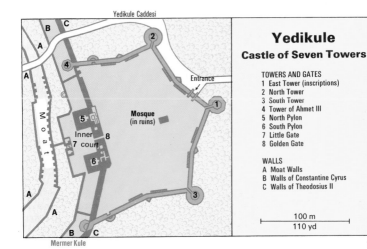

Yedikule
Castle of Seven Towers

TOWERS AND GATES
1 East Tower (inscriptions)
2 North Tower
3 South Tower
4 Tower of Ahmet III
5 North Pylon
6 South Pylon
7 Little Gate
8 Golden Gate

WALLS
A Moat Walls
B Walls of Constantine Cyrus
C Walls of Theodosius II

100 m
110 yd

Yedikule Caddesi

Entrance

Mosque
(in ruins)

Inner
court

Moat

Mermer Kule

Yedikule, the Castle of Seven Towers

*Yeni Camii (New Mosque)   D7

Location
Eminönü

Suburban railway station
Sirkeci

Bus stop
Eminönü

Boat landing-stage
Eminönü

The massive bulk of the Yeni Camii rears up at the south end of Galata Bridge. The mosque was originally founded in 1597 by the mother of Sultan Mehmet III, but in 1660, when still only half completed, it was destroyed by fire. Thereupon Mahmut IV's mother, Valide Sultan Turhan Hatice, had it rebuilt by the Court Architect, Mustafa Ağa. The new mosque was completed in 1663.

The Yeni Camii cruciform in plan. The main dome (36 m (118 ft) high, 17·5 m (57 ft) in diameter) is surrounded by four semi-domes, each supported by two smaller semi-domes. At the corners of the building are four small domes. The cascade of domes combines with the two slender minarets (each with three balconies and fine stalactitic work) to form a striking silhouette.

On the north and south fronts are two-storeyed galleries with porticoes.

Forecourt

The forecourt of the mosque, surrounded by arcades, resembles the atrium of a Byzantine church. The main gateway is richly decorated with tiles and columns of rare marble. In the centre of the court is a beautiful octagonal ablution fountain.

Interior

The interior is classical in style. The dome, borne on four massive piers, has 24 windows, which admit surprisingly little light. The walls are faced with tiles (green and blue on a white ground). The mihrab and mimber are in finely worked marble.

Yeni Camii (in background the Süleyman Mosque)

An unusual feature of the Yeni Camii is the loge of the Sultan's mother, at the east corner of the mosque. It is connected by a closed passageway with the beautifully appointed royal apartments (recently opened to the public as a museum: tiles, gold ornaments, intarsia work).

Loge of the Valide Sultan

Near the south corner of the mosque is the domed türbe of the founder, one of the largest in Istanbul, with the tombs of Turhan Hatice, her son Mehmet IV, Sultans Mustafa II, Ahmet III, Mahmut I, Osman III and Murat V, and various princesses and princes.

Türbe

Also within the mosque complex are the muvakkithane (clock-room) with an interesting roof structure, a fountain-house with beautiful marble walls and bronze screens and the Egyptian Bazaar (see Mısır Çarşısı).

Other buildings

*Yerebatan Sarayı (Underground Palace; Yerebatan Cistern)   D/E8

The Yerebatan Sarayı (Underground Palace), near the Hippodrome and Sultan Ahmet Square, is the largest and most impressive cistern in Istanbul. Constructed in the time of Justinian I (6th c.), it had a capacity of some 80,000 cu. m (18 million gallons) and was supplied by a 19 km (12 mile) long aqueduct from the Belgrade Forest (see Belgrat Ormanı).
The cistern is 140 m (460 ft) long and 70 m (230 ft) wide. The roof is supported by a forest of 336 8 m (26 ft) high columns set in 12 rows at intervals of 5 m (16 ft).

Location
Near At Meydanı

Bus stop
Sultanahmet

Opening times
Wed.–Mon. 9 a.m.–5 p.m.

Yerebatan Sarayı

Pond in Yıldız Parkı

*Yıldız Parkı (Star Park)

A11/12

Yıldız Parkı, the park of the 19th c. Yıldız Palace (Yıldız Sarayı), once the residence of Sultan Abdül Hamit II (opening it to the public as a museum is planned), lies on the slopes above the European shore of the Bosphorus between Beşiktaş and Ortaköy (see entries), offering wide views over the Bosphorus. A popular resort of the people of Istanbul, it is at present being re-landscaped.

At the lower entrance to the park is a small mosque built by Sultan Abdül Mecit in 1848–49. Just above the gate is a türbe containing 11 sarcophagi (mother-of-pearl inlay work), including that of Şeyh Yahya Efendi, a miraculous healer of the time of Süleyman the Magnificent.

From here paths lead up the hill to various attractive viewpoints, beautifully laid out gardens (rose-beds, winter garden, etc.) and three royal pavilions recently renovated by the Turkish Touring and Automobile Club, the Şale Köşkü, the Çadir Köşkü (collection of material on the Ottoman reforms of 1839) and the Malta Köşkü (café; various events). On the north-western side of the park stands a mosque built by Sultan Abdül Hamit II in 1886.

Location
European side of Bosphorus, between Beşiktaş and Ortaköy

Bus stops
Yıldız, Beşiktaş

Boat landing-stage
Beşiktas

Opening times
Daily 8.30 a.m.–5.30 p.m.

Zal Mahmut Paşa Camii

See Eyüp

*Zeyrek Camii (Zeyrek Mosque; Pantocrator Monastery)

D5

The Pantocrator Monastery, commandingly situated above Atatürk Bulvarı, was founded in the 12th c. by the Empress Irene, wife of John II Comnenus. The first buiding to be erected was the Pantocrator Church (south church), followed soon afterwards by a smaller church in similar style (north church). The two churches are linked by the burial chapel of the Comneni (used in the 15th c. by the Palaeologi), which was dedicated to the Archangel Michael. Around the churches were built a hospital, a school of medicine, monks' cells and various offices. During the political troubles at the beginning of the 13th c. the monastery was looted, and shortly afterwards it was taken over by Venetian clergy.

After the Conquest of Constantinople, Mehmet Fâtih converted the monastery into a medrese under the direction of Molla Mehmet Efendi, and soon afterwards it became a mosque. During the 18th c., the interior of the Pantocrator Church was remodelled, and most of the marble cladding and mosaic decoration was lost. Since the Second World War much work has been done to preserve the building and the surviving decoration.

The Pantocrator complex is attributed to the celebrated Byzantine architect Nicephorus. The Pantocrator Church (south church) and its companion north church are typical domed cruciform churches, each with three apses at the east

Location
Ibadethane Sok.

Bus stop
Zeyrek

Architecture

179

end. Squeezed in between the two churches is the burial chapel of the Comneni and Palaeologi. The three buildings are linked by a common narthex; the Pantocrator Church also has an exonarthex.

Interior

Fragments of a magnificent *opus sectile* pavement (representations of the Four Seasons, signs of the zodiac, Samson's fight with the lion, etc.) and of the marble cladding of the walls, traces of the mosaic decoration which probably covered the whole of the central area and a few panels of stained glass are all that remains of the churches' former splendours.

Practical Information

Airlines

Türk Hava Yolları (THY: Turkish Airlines)
Head office, Elmadağ, tel. 1 47 13 38
Yeşilköy Airport, tel. 5 73 73 60, 5 73 73 88, 6 73 71 54
City Terminal, Meşrutiyet Cad. 30, tel. 1 42 45 36
Flight information: tel. 1 44 02 96
Reservations: tel. 1 45 70 55

British Airways
Cumhuriyet Cad. 10, tel. 1 48 42 35–38

PanAm
Hilton Methali Harbiye, tel. 1 47 45 30

Airport (Hava alanı)

Istanbul's Yeşilköy International Airport (tel. 5 73 73 99) lies 18 km (11 miles) west of the city centre. There are regular bus services between the airport and the city terminal (THY Terminal, Meşrutiyet Cad. 26, Şişhane).

Antiques

See Shopping

Banks

Mon.–Fri. 8.30 a.m.–5 p.m. — Opening times

In most banks in the city centre Eurocheques and Travelers checks can be cashed and money changed. Regard should be had to the currency regulations (see Currency) and to the different rates offered by banks. — Eurocheques/ Travelers checks

Sirkeci Station: Sat. 9 a.m.–12 noon
Yeşilköy Airport: throughout the day
Principal hotels: throughout the day — Changing money at weekends and on public holidays

Beware of offers to change money in the street. This is illegal, and involves the additional risk of getting counterfeit currency in exchange. — Changing money privately

Beaches

	There are numerous bathing beaches along both the European and the Asiatic sides of the Sea of Marmara.
European side	West-south-west of the city centre are the beaches of Ataköy, Yeşilköy and Florya.
Asiatic side	South of Üsküdar are the beaches of Moda, Fenerbahçe, Caddebostan and Suadiye.
Princes' Islands	Bathing beaches and coves on all the larger islands.
Black Sea	There are two excellent sandy bathing beaches on the Black Sea, at Kilyos on the European side (west of the mouth of the Bosphorus) and at Şile on the Asiatic side (east of the mouth of the Bosphorus).

Bus stations (Otobüs Terminalı)

European side	Topkapı Otobüs Terminalı, outside the walls at the point where E 5 enters the city, buses to Thrace and Antatolia.
	Sultanahmet Terminalı, Sultanahmet Meydanı, long-distance buses to Europe and Asia.
Asiatic side	Harem Otobüs Terminalı, at ship landing-stage, Harem İskelesi, buses to Anatolia.

Camping sites (Kamplar)

Ataköy Camping
on coast road, at Bakırköy, tel. 5 72 35 42

Kervansaray Kartaltepe Mocamp
at Yeşilköy Airport, Çobançeşme, tel. 5 71 21 50

Yeşilyurt Camping, Sahil Yolu Cad.,
on coast road to Yeşilköy, tel. 5 73 84 08

Car rental (Oto kiralama acentalari)

Esin (Europcar, National Car Rental)
Cumhuriyet Cad. 47/2, tel. 1 44 01 90

Kaynan
Hotel Etap Marmara, Taksim, tel. 1 45 07 56

Setur
Cumhuriyet Cad. 107, Harbiye, tel. 1 48 50 85

Kontuar
Cumhuriyet Cad. 283, Harbiye, tel. 1 47 31 40

Chemists (Eczaneler)

Current products of the Western pharmaceutical industry are available in most chemists' shops without prescription.

Chemists' shops are usually open on weekdays from 9 a.m. to 1 p.m. and 2 to 7 p.m.

Opening times

Duty doctors and chemists: dial 01

Emergencies

Churches and Religious Meeting Places (Kiliseler)

Sant'Antonio di Padova
İstiklâl Cad. 327, Tünel

Roman Catholic

Saint-Esprit (Notre Dame de Sion Lisesi)
Cumhuriyet Cad. 205, Elmadağ

St Louis (chapel of French Consulate)
İstiklâl Cad. 8, Beyoğlu

St Mary Draperis
İstiklâl Cad. 429, Galatasaray

Aynalıçeşme, Galatasaray

Protestant

Neve Shalom
at Galata Tower, Şişhane

Synagogue

Coffee-house (Kahve)

The coffee-house, where men meet to exchange the news of the day, drink coffee and play the national game, tavla (backgammon), is found everywhere. Visitors will often see men smoking the traditional water-pipe (nargile) in a coffee-house.

Consulates (Konsoloshaneler)

Tepebaşı, Meşrutiyet Cad. 34, tel. 1 44 75 40

United Kingdom

Meşrutiyet Cad. 104, tel. 1 43 62 00–09

United States

Currency/Currency Regulations

The unit of currency is the Turkish lira (TL). There are banknotes for 5, 10, 20, 50, 100, 500, 1000 and 5000 TL and coins in denominations of 1, 2, 5, 10, 20 and 50 TL.

Import and export of currency

There is no limit on the amount of foreign currency that may be taken into Turkey, but not more than $1000-worth of Turkish currency may be taken into or out of the country.

Exchange receipts

All exchange receipts for the conversion of foreign currency into Turkish money should be kept, since you may be required to produce them when reconverting your Turkish money and when taking souvenirs out of the country (in order to show that your Turkish money was obtained by legal exchange).

Cheques

Eurocheques can be cashed immediately, as can traveller's cheques upon producing identification. It may take several days to cash cheques drawn on private accounts.

Credit cards

The major credit cards are accepted by the larger hotels, expensive shops and car hire firms, and their use is gradually spreading.

Customs regulations

Entry

Only a verbal declaration is required when entering Turkey.
The following items may be taken into the country without payment of duty:
personal effects, clothing and jewellery (but not furs); books and magazines, a portable typewriter, a transistor radio, a camera and up to 10 films, a musical instrument and necessary medical supplies.
Items of particular value may be entered in the visitor's passport, so that the customs authorities can check that they are re-exported.
In addition there are duty-free allowances of 400 cigarettes, 50 cigars, 200 grams of tobacco, 1 kg of coffee, 500 grams of instant coffee, 1 kg of tea and five bottles of spirits, of which no more than three may be of the same brand.
Sharp instruments (including camping knives) and weapons may not be taken into the country without special authority.
The import, trade in and use of marijuana and all other narcotics is strictly prohibited and subject to heavy penalties.
Gifts not exceeding £150 ($225) in value may be taken in duty-free.

Leaving Turkey

Gifts and souvenirs up to the value of 15,000 TL may be taken out of the country without formality. For a new carpet proof of purchase must be produced; for old carpets, copper articles and pistols a certificate of authority from a museum is required.
The export of antiques is prohibited.
Valuable personal items can be taken out of the country if they have been recorded in the owner's passport on entry into Turkey, or can be proved to have been bought with legally exchanged currency.

Dolmus

See Taxis

Earthquakes

Istanbul lies in a zone subject to quite frequent earthquakes, sometimes very severe (7 on the Richter scale).

Electricity

Normally 220 volts throughout Turkey; occasionally 110 volts in European Turkey and Istanbul. In hotels the voltage is marked on all sockets.
Plugs have two round prongs, usually of the smaller European diameter. An adaptor should be taken for an electric razor, etc.

Emergencies

Police, ambulance:
All parts of the city: tel. 1 66 66 66
Stamboul: tel. 5 21 15 95
Taksim: tel. 1 44 49 98
Üsküdar: tel. 3 33 04 01

Fire:
Stamboul: tel. 55 24 11
Beyoğlu/Taksim: tel. 1 40 77 77
Üsküdar: tel. 3 33 20 30

Hospitals: see that entry

Medical Emergency: tel. 01

Events

Tulip Festival, Emirgân	April/May
Istanbul Festival (music, theatre, ballet, folk events)	Mid June–mid July
Textile Fair	July
International Festival, Bursa (music and theatre)	
Troy Festival, Çanakkale	August
Trade Fair of the Islamic Countries	November
Textile Fair	
Furniture Fair	December
Son et lumière performances (Topkapı Sarayı, Ayasofya, Sultan Ahmet Camii, Rumeli Hisarı)	May–October

Practical Information

Excursions

Excursions to places around Istanbul can be booked in most travel agencies and hotels (see entries).

Boat trips

There are attractive trips from Eminönü harbour station (south end of Galata Bridge) along the Bosphorus, to the Princes' Islands and to Yalova. There are cruises along the Golden Horn from Yemiş İskelesi (west of the south end of Galata Bridge).

Coach trips

There are coach trips (usually lasting two or three days) to İznik, Bursa, Çanakkale and Troy. Particularly worth while is a three-day tour to Bursa, Çanakkale and Troy, with a crossing of the Dardanelles.

By rail

Ankara and Edirne are best visited by train. Both cities are served by frequent main-line services. Fares are relatively low; children under 7 travel free. Trains to Ankara leave from Haydarpaşa Station (Asiatic side), trains to Edirne from Sirkeci (European side).

Food and drink

The cuisine of Istanbul is noted for the purity and quality of the ingredients and careful preparation to traditional recipes, producing a wide variety of tasty dishes. The people prefer a fresh and unadulterated taste rather than the use of elaborate spices and seasonings.

Arnavut ciğeri	Pieces of liver, fried, with onion rings
Aşure	A pudding of boiled wheat grains, raisins, dried figs, beans and nuts
Baklava	Flaky pastry with walnut or pistachio stuffing
Balık yumurtası	Fish roe
Beyaz peynir	Goat's-milk cheese
Biber dolması	Stuffed peppers
Bonfile	Steak
Bulgur pilav	Cracked wheat pilaf
Cacık	A salad of grated cucumber, yoghurt and garlic
Çerkes tavuğu	Chicken in a walnut and paprika sauce
Çiğ köfte	Highly seasoned meat-balls
Çoban salatası	Mixed salad of tomatoes, cucumbers and onions
Döner kebab	Lamb or mutton roasted on a vertical spit
Dondurma	Ice-cream
Düğün çorbası	"Wedding soup": lamb soup flavoured with lemon juice and thickened with beaten eggs
Ekmek	Bread
Fasulye piyaz	Salad of dried beans with onion rings and hard-boiled eggs
Güllaç	Waffles stuffed with ground almonds and dipped in milk
Hamsi tavası	Fried anchovies

Hünkâr beğendi	"The Sultan likes it": meat goulash with purée of aubergines
Hurma tatlısı	Date pudding
İç pilav	Chopped chicken-liver pilaf, with spices, raisins and pistachios or pine seeds
İmam bayıldı	"The imam fainted": aubergines with onions and tomatoes in olive oil, served cold
İşkembe çorbası	Mutton tripe soup
Kabak dolması	Vegetable marrow with a rice and meat stuffing
Kabak kızartması	Fried marrow slices, served with yoghurt
Kabak tatlısı	Marrow boiled with sugar, sprinkled with grated nuts
Kadın budu	"Lady's thigh": lamb and rice croquettes
Kadın göbeği	"Lady's navel": doughnut soaked in syrup
Kılıç şiş	Swordfish roasted on the spit
Kuzu dolması	Grilled lamb with savoury rice
Midye dolması	Stuffed mussels
Patlıcan kızartması	Fried aubergine slices, served with yoghurt
Pirzola	Lamb cutlet
Piyaz	Bean salad
Revâni	Semolina pudding
Sarığı burma	A rich flaky dessert with nut filling
Şiş kebab	Grilled pieces of lamb
Şiş köfte	Grilled meat-balls
Su böreği	A pasty filled with minced meat and grated cheese
Sütlaç	Rice pudding
Tarama	Fish roe
Tel kadayıf	A sweet pastry filled with walnuts or pistachios and soaked in syrup
Tütün balık	Smoked fish
Vezir parmağı	"Vizier's finger": a baked sweet pudding
Yaprak dolması	Stuffed vine leaves
Zerde	Saffron rice pudding
Zeytinyağlı fasculye	String beans cooked in olive oil, with tomato sauce

Fruit:

Erik	Plum
İncir	Fig
Karpuz	Water melon
Kavun	Melon
Kayısı	Apricot
Kiraz	Cherry
Şeftali	Peach
Üzüm	Grapes
Zeytin	Olive

Drinks:

Çay	Tea, the national drink. In summer tea-gardens are a favourite resort. Tea is frequently served in a samovar.

Ayran	Yoghurt, mixed with water and slightly salted.
Raki	A spirit distilled from grapes with an aniseed flavour.
Bira	Beer. The local beer is very light, and when in good condition is extremely palatable.
Şarap	Wine, which is not much drunk in Turkey. Well-known brands are Doluca (red and white), Kavaklıdere (red and white), Yakut Damlas (red) and Lâl (rose).
Kahve	Coffee, which in Turkey is relatively dear. In good coffee-houses Turkish coffee is made on a side table in the client's presence.

Getting to Istanbul

By air

There are daily flights to Istanbul from London Heathrow by British Airways and Turkish Airlines.
PanAm have direct flights to Istanbul from various cities in the United States.

By car

The distance from London to Istanbul by road is about 3000 km (1800–1900 miles).
Recommended routes: Calais or Ostend to Brussels, Cologne and Frankfurt; then either via Nuremberg, Linz, Vienna, Budapest and Belgrade or Stuttgart, Munich, Salzburg, Ljubljana, Zagreb and Belgrade; and from Belgrade via Niš, Sofia and Edirne to Istanbul. An alternative possibility is to drive from Munich to Venice or Ancona and take the car ferry to Istanbul.
Car documents required: driving licence (international driving licence preferable); car registration document; "green card" (international insurance certificate) or Turkish third-party insurance taken out at the frontier.
Personal documents: in addition to the normal passport, transit visas will be required for the journey through Yugoslavia (not for British citizens) and Bulgaria.

By bus

There are no direct bus services from London to Istanbul, but there are Europabus services from Geneva, Munich and Vienna, and services run by Turkish companies from Paris and Metz.

Information and reservations, Europabus services:

Sealink,
Room 27, Eversholt House,
163–203 Eversholt Street,
London NW1 1BG, tel. (01) 388 6846

British Rail Travel Centre,
12 Regent Street,
London SW1
(personal callers only)

Information on other services:
Turkish Office of Tourism (see Information)

The journey by rail to Istanbul is very long and slow. It can also be interrupted by unscheduled stops. There is no through service from London, but it is possible to connect with services from Dortmund (Hellas–Istanbul Express), Munich (Istanbul Express, Tauern–Orient Express), Venice (Istanbul Express) and Vienna (Istanbul Express, Balkan Express).
The old Orient Express no longer runs to Istanbul except on special (and expensive) excursions.

By rail

Information:
British Rail Travel Centre,
12 Regent Street,
London SW1
(personal callers only)
and British Rail information offices at major stations

Health

Required for visitors coming from Asia and Africa (except Morocco).

Smallpox vaccination

Required only for visitors coming from areas where cholera is prevalent.

Cholera vaccination

Hospitals (Hastaneler)

Amiral Bristol Amerikan Hastanesi
Güzelbahçe Sok., Nisantaşi
tel. 1 48 60 30

American hospital

Pasteur Fransız Hastanesi
Divan Hotel Arkası, Taksim
tel. 1 48 47 56

French hospitals

La Paix Hastanesi
Büyükdere Cad., Şişli
tel. 1 48 18 32

Alman Hastanesi
Sıraselviler Cad., Taksim
tel. 1 43 55 00

German hospital

Hotels (Oteller)

A selection:

Çirağan, Müvezzi Cad. 3, 102 beds	Beşiktaş
Akgün, Ordu Cad./Haznedar Sok. 6, 153 beds	Beyazit
Sözmen, Millet Cad. 258, 125 beds	Çapa
Plaza, Aslanyatağı Sok. 19–21, 60 beds	Cihangir
Dragos, Dragos Sahilyolu, 126 beds	Cevizli/Kartal

Practical Information

Esentepe

Dedeman,Yıldızposta Cad. 50, 542 beds

Fındıkzade

Anka, Mollagüran Cad. 42, 130 beds
Topkapı, Oğuzhan Cad. 20, 80 beds

Gayrettepe

TMT, Büyükdere Cad., 199 beds

Harbiye

*Divan, Cumhuriyet Cad., 191 beds
*Hilton, Cumhuriyet Cad., 770 beds

Harem

Harem Üsküdar Selimiye, 204 beds

Lâleli/Aksaray

Büyük Keban, Gençtürk Cad. 41–47, 271 beds
Cidde, Aksaray Cad. 10, 126 beds
Dorn, Gençtürk Cad. 44, 50 beds
München, Gençtürk Cad. 55, 40 beds
Toro, Koska Cad. 24, 102 beds

Şehzadebası

Barin, Fevziye Cad. 25, 54 beds
Maya, Fevziye Cad. 19–21, 66 beds

Şile

Değirmen, Plajyolu 24, 149 beds

Sirkeci

İpek Palas, Orhaniye Cad. 9, 66 beds

Suadiye

Suadiye, Plajyolu Sok. 51, 215 beds

Sultanahmet

Kalyon, Sahilyolu, 76 beds

Taksim

*Etap Marmara, Taksim Meydanı, 704 beds
*Sheraton, Taksim Parkı, 855 beds
Dilson, Sıraselviler Cad. 43, 180 beds
Gezi, Mete Cad. 42, 66 beds
Keban, Sıraselviler Cad. 51, 160 beds
Kennedy, Sıraselviler Cad. 79, 60 beds
Opera, İnönü Cad. 38–42, 97 beds
Park, İnönü Cad. 6, 80 beds
Santral, Sıraselviler Cad. 26, 202 beds
Star, Sağlik Sok. 11–13, 48 beds

Tarabya

*Büyük Tarabya, Kefeliköy, 524 beds

Tepebaşi

Etap İstanbul, Meşrutiyet Cad., 370 beds
Pera Palas, Meşrutiyet Cad., 200 beds
Kavak, Meşrutiyet Cad. 201–203, 70 beds
Yenişehir, Meşrutiyet Cad./Balyoz Sok. 3/1, 84 beds

Teşvikiye

Maçka, Eytam Cad. 35, 361 beds

Topkapı

Olcay, Millet Cad. 187, 256 beds

Yalova

Gökçedere, Gökçedere Köyü, 86 beds

Yeniköy

Carlton, Köybaşı Cad., 242 beds

Yeşilköy

*Çınar, Yeşilköy, 402 beds

See also Youth Hostels

Information (Enformasyon)

Turkish Tourism and Information Office
170–173 Piccadilly (first floor),
London W1V 9DD
tel. (01) 734 8681–82

In the United Kingdom

Turkish Tourism and Information Office
821 United Nations Plaza,
New York NY 10017
tel. (212) 687 2194

In the United States

Information Bureaux (Turizm Danisma) of Ministry of Culture
and Tourism:

In Istanbul

Meşrutiyet Cad. 57, Galatasaray
tel. 1 45 68 75

Karaköy landing-stage (passenger reception hall)
tel. 1 49 57 76

Hilton Hotel
tel. 1 40 68 64

Sultanahmet Square
tel. 5 22 49 03

Yeşilköy Airport
tel. 5 73 73 99

Municipal Information Bureaux (Belediye Enformasyon
Büroları):

Town Hall, Saraçhane Meydanı
tel. 5 26 21 00

Covered Bazaar, at Bedesten
tel. 5 27 00 04

Sirkeci Station
tel. 5 27 42 32

Haydarpaşa Station
tel. 3 36 36 79

Kabataş landing-stage
tel. 1 49 19 16

Language

Turkish is an agglutinative language, quite different from any
European language, in which words are built up by the addition
of one or more suffixes to the root. Another distinctive feature
is vowel harmony, which means that all the vowels in a word
must be either front vowels (e, i, ö, ü) or back vowels (a, ı, o, u),
the various suffixes being modified to match the vowels of the

Practical Information

root; there are some exceptions to this rule, mainly in words of Arabic or other non-Turkish origin.

One suffix frequently used is the -i (modified to -ı, -u or -ü) or, after a vowel -si (-si, -su, -sü) used on nouns modified by other nouns or pronouns and in possessives. The *cami* is a mosque, but when modified by a noun it becomes *camii* (e.g. Fethiye Camii); when modified by an adjective it takes no suffix (Yeni Cami, the New Mosque).

Fortunately visitors to Istanbul will be able to find many Turks with at least a smattering of English, French or particularly German.

Alphabet:

Turkish	Pronunciation
a	*a*
b	*b*
c	*j*
ç	*ch* as in "church"
d	*d*
e	*e*
f	*f*
g	*g* (hard, as in "gag")
ğ	(barely perceptible; lengthens preceding vowel)
h	*h* (emphatically pronounced, approaching *ch* in "loch")
ı	a dark *uh* sound
i	*i*
j	*zh* as in "pleasure"
k	*k*
l	*l*
m	*m*
n	*n*
o	*o*
ö	*eu*, as in French "deux"
p	*p*
r	*r*
s	*s*
ş	*sh*
t	*t*
u	*u*
ü	as in French "une"
v	*v*
y	*y*, as in "yet"
z	*z*

Numbers:

0	sıfır
1	bir
2	iki
3	üç
4	dört
5	beş
6	altı
7	yedi
8	sekiz
9	dokuz
10	on
11	on bir
20	yirmi

21	yirmi bir
30	otuz
40	kırk
50	elli
60	altmış
70	yetmiş
80	seksen
90	doksan
100	yüz
200	iki yüz
1000	bin

Fractions:

$\frac{1}{2}$	yarım
$\frac{1}{4}$	çeyrek

Topographical and technical terms:

ada	island
bahçe	island
bedesten	market hall
cadde	street
cami	mosque
çarşı	bazaar, market
çeşme	(drinking) fountain
darüşşifa	hospital
dershane	schoolroom
göl	lake
hamam	bath-house
han	inn; large commercial building
hisar	castle, fortress
imâret	public kitchen (attached to a mosque)
iskele	boat landing-stage
kale	fortress
kapı	gate
kemer	arch of a bridge
kervansaray	caravanserai
kıbla wall	wall in a mosque indicating direction of Mecca
kilise	church
köşk	pavilion, kiosk
köy	village
kule	tower
külliye	mosque complex
Kuran kürsü	chair in a mosque from which the imam reads from the Koran
kütüphane	library
liman	harbour
maksure	private pew in a mosque
medrese	theological school
mektep	primary school
mihrab	niche in a mosque indicating the direction of Mecca
mimber	pulpit
muvakkithane	clock-house, clock-room of a mosque
müze	museum
oda	room
revak	colonnade round a courtyard
şadirvan	ablution fountain
şaray	palace
sebil	fountain-house

sofa	hall, anteroom; stone bench, sofa
sokak	street
tabhane	hostel, hospice
tekke	dervish convent
tepe	hill
türbe	mausoleum
yalı	mansion on the Bosphorus, summer-house
yol	road

Libraries

Many libraries in Istanbul, including some belonging to foreign cultural or learned bodies, have old manuscripts, valuable old books and modern publications of all kinds. Many of them are not normally open to the public or can be seen only by appointment. For information apply to the official information bureaux (see Information).

Lost property offices (Kayıp eşya müracaat büroları)

Experience has shown that in a large cosmopolitan city like Istanbul the prospects of recovering lost property are not good. The following agencies can be applied to:

Town Hall

Belediye Sarayı, Saraçhane Meydanı, Saraçhane, tel. 5 26 21 00

Transport Department

IETT Genel Müdürlüğü, Metrohan, Tünel, tel. 1 46 81 31

Railway stations

Sirkeci İstasyonu, tel. 5 27 00 51
Haydarpaşa İstasyonu, tel. 3 36 20 63

Harbour station

Deniz Yolları, Karaköy, tel. 1 49 71 78

Airport

Yeşilköy Hava Alanı, tel. 5 73 73 60

Markets

See Shopping

Motoring

Traffic regulations

Speed limits:
in built-up areas 50 km p.h. (31 m.p.h.);
outside built-up areas 90 km p.h. (56 m.p.h.);
cars with trailers 80 km p.h. (50 m.p.h.);
motor-cycles 70 km p.h. (43 m.p.h.)
Seat-belts must be worn.
It is an offence to drive after drinking *any* alcohol.
Two warning triangles must be carried, to be set up both in front of and behind the vehicle in case of accident or breakdown.
In case of an accident incurring damage to the car, a police report is essential.

The directions given by police or military personnel must be
obeyed implicitly.

Türkiye Turing ve Otomobil Kurumu (TTOK)   Automobile Club
Halâskargazi Cad. 384, Şişli, tel. 1 46 70 90

Road patrols are operated by the Turing Servisi on the Edirne–   Road patrols
Istanbul–Ankara and Edirne–Istanbul–Izmir roads.

Tel. 1 46 70 90 or 5 21 65 88 (only during the day).   Breakdown assistance
There are charges for turning out and for assistance given.

All the main car manufacturers have authorised garages (for   Service garages
servicing and repairs) in Istanbul. In addition there are any
number of smaller garages and workshops.

For police or ambulance from anywhere in Istanbul   Emergency calls
dial 1 66 66 66.

Museums

Alay Köşkü Müzesi
See A to Z, Alay Köskü

Arasta Mozaik Müzesi (Mosaic Museum)
See A to Z, Arasta Mozaik Müzesi

Arkeoloji Müzesi (Archaeological Museum)
See A to Z, Arkeoloji Müzesi

Askeri Müzesi (Military Museum)
See A to Z, Askeri Müzesi

Atatürk Müzesi (Atatürk Museum)
See A to Z, Atatürk Müzesi

Aya İrini Müzesi (Haghia Eirene Church)
See Aya İrini Kilisesi

Ayasofya Müzesi (Haghia Sophia)
See A to Z, Ayasofya

Belediye Müzesi (Municipal Museum)
See A to Z, Belediye Müzesi

Carpet Museum
See A to Z, Sultan Ahmet Camii

Deniz Müzesi (Maritime Museum)
See A to Z, Deniz Müzesi

Dolmabahçe Sarayı (Dolmabahçe Palace)
See A to Z, Dolmabahçe Sarayı

Eski Şark Eserleri Müzesi (Museum of the Ancient Orient)
See A to Z, Arkeoloji Müzesi, Eski Şark Eserleri Müzesi

Practical Information

Eski Yazı Sanatları Müzesi (Museum of Calligraphy)
Sultan Selim Medresesi, Vatan Cad.
Open Tues.–Sat. 9 a.m.–5 p.m.

Galata Mevlevihane Müzesi (Divan Museum)
See A to Z, Galta Mevlevihane Müzesi

Kariye Müzesi (St Saviour in Chora)
See A to Z, Kariye Camii

Resim ve Heykel Müzesi (Museum of Modern Art)
See A to Z, Resim ve Heykel Müzesi

Rumeli Hisarı Müzesi (Fortress of Rumeli Hisarı)
See A to Z, Rumeli Hisarı

Tanzimat Müzesi (Tanzimat Memorial Museum)
Nüzhetiye Cad., Meşrutiyet
Open Tues.–Fri. 9 a.m.–4 p.m.

Topkapı Sarayı Müzesi (Topkapı Palace)
See A to Z, Topkapı Sarayı

Türk İnşaat Sanatları Müzesi (Building Museum)
See A to Z, Amcazade Hüseyin Pasa Medresesi

Türk ve Islâm Eserleri Müzesi (Museum of Turkish and Islamic Art)
See A to Z, Türk ve Islâm Eserleri Müzesi

Yedikule Müzesi
See A to Z, Yedikule

Yerebatan Müzesi (Yerebatan Cistern)
See A to Z, Yerebatan Sarayı

Music

Opera, ballet, concerts

Atatürk Kültür Merkezi (Opera House)
Taksim Meydanı

Folk performances

Topkapı Sarayı
Açik Hava Tiyatrosu, Taşkişla Cad., Maçka
Rumeli Hisarı
Ayasofya Meydanı
Sultanahmet Meydanı

Istanbul Festival

The famous Istanbul Festival (opera, drama, ballet and concerts with a very varied programme and artistes of international standing) takes place from mid June to mid July.

Night life

Night spots
(a selection; some with belly-dancing)

Foliberjer, Beşir Fuad Cad. 8, Tepebaşı
Open until 1 a.m.

Galata Kulesi Night Club, Galata Tower, Şişhane
Open until midnight

Kervansaray, Cumhuriyet Cad. 30, Elmadağ
Open until midnight

Lunapark, Vatan Cad. 79, Aksaray

Maksim, Caddebostan
Open until 1 a.m.

Pariziyen, Cumhuriyet Cad. 18, Elmadağ
Open until 1 a.m.

Pembe Köşk, Kennedy Cad. 38, Sahilyolu
Open 9 p.m. to 12.30 a.m.

Siesta, Sıraselviler Cad. 61, Taksim
Open 9 p.m. to 1.30 a.m.

Ceneviz Meyhanesi, in Galata Tower
Open 7.30 p.m. to 1 a.m.

Bars
(a selection; excludes hotel bars)

Tadal, Ergenekon Cad. 79, Pangaltı
Open noon to 8 p.m.

Valentino, Sıraselviler Cad. 63
Open 6 p.m. to 2 a.m.

Club 33, Cumhuriyet Cad. 18, Elmadağ
Open 9 p.m. to 1 a.m.

Discothèques
(a selection)

Disco 2000, Sheraton Hotel, Taksim
Open 10 p.m. to 1.15 a.m.

Hydromel, Cumhuriyet Cad. 12, Elmadağ
Open 9 p.m. to 1 a.m.

Regine, Cumhuriyet Cad. 16, Elmadağ
Open 9 p.m. to 1 a.m.

Topkapı, Hotel Etap İstanbul, Tepebaşı
Open 9 p.m. to 5 a.m.

A visit to a belly-dancing (or Oriental dancing) show is highly recommended for every tourist in Istanbul. The belly dance, performed in the past by amply proportioned dancers but now usually by slim and shapely young women, had its origins in sequences of movements executed in the course of fertility rites in Africa and southern Asia. Its main features are a rolling movement of the pelvis and the rhythmic contraction of the stomach muscles. Performed in accordance with ancient traditions, the classical and artistic movements of the dancer's body are accompanied by Near Eastern music (with drums and the clarinet predominating). The dancer herself may contribute to the accompaniment with bells which are either hung round her hips or held in her hands.

Belly-dancing

Practical Information

Sulukule

In the poorer quarters of the city along the land walls (near the Mihrimah Mosque and the Edirne Gate), occupied by many gipsy familes, the more venturesome visitor will find numbers of night spots in which girls, mostly very young, perform in uninhibited dancing or striptease shows to deafening music.

Entertainments quarter

See A to Z, İstiklâl Caddesi

Opening times

Shops and Markets

Weekdays 9 a.m.–1 p.m. and 2–7 p.m. (though many do not close at lunchtime).

Public and Government offices and banks

Mon.–Fri. 8.30 or 9 a.m. to 5 p.m.
Some offices close at lunchtime.

Post offices

Mon.–Sat. 8 a.m.–5 p.m.; head post offices in Aksaray, Beyoğlu, Kadıköy and Sirkeci Mon.–Sat. 8 a.m.–midnight, Sun. 9 a.m.–7 p.m.

Museums

Most museums are open between 9 a.m. and 4.30 p.m., but weekly holidays, lunchtime breaks and late opening arrangements vary widely. Enquire of the official information bureaux (see Information).

Parking garages (Kapalı oto parkları)

Aksaray Akın Garajı
Harikzadeler Sok. 2, Lâleli

Etap Marmara
Etap Marmara Hotel, Taksim Square, Taksim

Karaköy Kat Otoparkı
Harbour Station, Karaköy

Şişli Çukurova Garajı
at Şişli Mosque

Taksim Opera Garajı
at Opera House, Taksim Square

Taksim Sheraton Oteli
Sheraton Hotel, Mete Cad., Elmadağ

Police (Polis)

Tourist police

Turizm Plisi, Sultanahmet, tel. 5 28 53 69

Police stations

There are police stations in all city districts and at important traffic intersections (e.g. Taksim, Eminönü, Topkapı).

Stamboul, tel. 5 21 15 95
Beyoğlu, tel. 1 44 49 98
Üsküdar, tel. 3 33 04 01

Main police stations

Tel. 05

Military police

Postal services (PTT)

Post offices are usually open on weekdays from 8 a.m. to 5 p.m.; the head post offices in Aksaray, Beyoğlu, Kadıköy and Sirkeci are open Mon.–Sat. from 8 a.m. to midnight, sun. 9 a.m.–7 p.m.

Post office opening times

Aksaray, Atatürk Bulvarı, tel. 5 26 51 94
Beyoğlu, Galatasaray, tel. 1 43 31 61
Kadıköy, near Harbour Station, tel. 3 37 05 16
Sirkeci, Eminönü, tel. 5 26 62 20

Head post offices

Poste restante mail should be addressed to one of the head post offices, marked "postrestant". It can be collected on presentation of passport.

Poste restante

See Telephone and telegrams

Telephone

Public holidays

Official holidays:
New Year's Day

1 January

National Independence Day and Children's Day

23 April

Youth and Sport Day; Atatürk Commemoration

19 May

Victory Day (commemorating victory over the Greeks in 1922)

30 August

Republic Day (anniversary of the declaration of the Turkish Republic)

29 October

Religious holidays:
There are two Islamic festivals recognised as public holidays: Şeker Bayramı (Sugar Festival), a three-day festival at the end of the Ramadan (in Turkish Ramazan) fast, and Kurban Bayramı, the four-day Festival of Sacrifice, on which sheep are slaughtered and distributed to the poor. The dates of these festivals are determined by the Islamic (lunar) calendar, and move ten days back each year. Shops and offices are closed on the days of the festival.

Public transport

There are suburban railway services (electric) between Sirkeci Station and the suburbs of Ataköy and Florya (beaches and camping sites) on the European side of the Sea of Marmara and between Haydarpaşa Station and suburbs on the Asiatic side.

Suburban railway

Practical Information

Buses

Travelling on the city (IETT) buses is cheap and easy. There is an excellent network of services, though journeys tend to take a long time. The main bus routes on the European side run via Taksim Square, Eminönü Square (at the Galata Bridge) and Hürriyet Square (near the Bazaar); on the Asiatic side they operate to and from the landing-stages at Üsküdar and Kadıküy.

Airport bus service

There is a shuttle service of buses between Yeşilköy Airport and the THY (Turkish Airlines) terminal in Şişhane.

Taxis, dolmuşes

See Taxis

Tünel funicular

The underground funicular known as the Tünel runs between the harbour quarter and the south end of İstiklâl Caddesi.

Boat services

Istanbul's boat services are convenient, pleasant and cheap. Boats to the Bosphorus, Golden Horn, Üsküdar, Kadıköy, Haydarpaşa (railway station on Asiatic side) and the Princes' Islands leave from the quays at the Galata Bridge (Köprü, "the Bridge").

Boat services:
Köprü–Beykos–Kavaklar
Köprü–Haydarpaşa–Kadıköy
Köprü–Üsküdar
Köprü–Harem
Kabataş–Adalar (Princes' Islands)
Eminönü–Adalar
Kabataş–Yalova
Kartal–Yalova
Bostancı–Köprü
Adalar–Bostancı
Köprü–Eyüp

There are car ferries between Kapataş and Üsküdar and between Sirkeci and Harem. The crossing takes about 20 minutes in each case.

Radio

There are news bulletins in English and French on the Third Programme of TRT, the Turkish Radio Corporation, daily at 12 noon and 5, 7 and 10 p.m.

Rail travel

See Excursions

Railway stations (İstasyonlar)

European side

Sirkeci İstasyonu
Information about services to European cities:
tel. 5 27 00 50–51
Reservations: tel. 5 27 59 84

Haydarpaşa İstasyonu
Information about services within Turkey and long-distance
services to destinations in Asia: tel. 3 36 04 75, 3 36 20 63
Reservations: tel. 3 36 44 70

Restaurants (Lokantalar)

Times given are for last service of hot meals; days given are
those on which the restaurant is closed.

°Abdullah, Mektep Cad. 11, Emirgân, tel. 1 63 64 06 (11 p.m.,
Tues.)
Four Seasons, İstiklâl Cad. 509, Tünel, tel. 1 45 89 41 (11 p.m.,
Sun.)
°Galata Kulesi, Şişhane, tel. 1 45 11 60 (1 a.m.)
Liman, at Karaköy Harbour Station, tel. 1 44 10 33 (4 p.m.)
Merih Şarap Mahzeni, Kuruçeşme Cad. 24/1, Arnavutköy,
tel. 1 63 59 77 (midnight)
Pizzeria Papillon, Akatlar 50, Yıl Çarşısı 21, Etiler, tel. 1 65 51 14
(midnight)
Rejans, Oliviya geç. 15, Galatasaray, tel. 1 44 16 10 (11 p.m.;
Russian specialities)
Swiss Pub, Cumhuriyet Cad. 14, Elmadağ, tel. 1 49 80 49
(11 p.m.)
Union Française, Meşrutiyet Cad. 233, Tepebaşı, tel. 1 44 43 64
(12.30 a.m.)

International cuisine

Garaj, Yeniköy Cad. 30, Tarabya, tel. 1 62 00 32 (midnight)
°Hacı Baba, İstiklâl Cad. 49, Taksim, tel. 1 44 18 86 (11 p.m.)
Ilyas, Merter, Londra Asfaltı, tel. 5 75 47 63 (11 p.m.)
Koco, İskele Yanı, Moda, tel. 3 36 07 95 (11 p.m.)
°Pandelli, Mısır Çarşısı, Eminönü, tel. 5 27 39 09 (3.30 p.m.)
°Sofra, Nuruosmaniye Cad. 10, Cağaloğlu, tel. 5 28 36 30
(11 p.m.)
Sarmasık, Büyük Tarabya, tel. 1 62 11 24 (1 a.m.)
Yalı, Köybası Cad. 235A, Yeniköy, tel. 1 62 12 88 (10 p.m.)

Turkish cuisine

Antik, Birinci Cad. 47, Arnavutköy, tel. 1 63 66 27 (1 a.m.)
Canlı Balık, Sahilyolu 101, Kumkapı, tel. 1 62 00 71 (midnight)
Caparı, Çaparı Sok. 22, Kumkapı, tel. 5 22 72 57 (midnight)
°Doganay, Yaliboyu Cad. 26, Beylerbeyi, tel. 3 33 01 97
(1 a.m.)
Facyo, Kireçburun, Tarabya Cad. 13, tel. 1 62 00 24 (midnight)
°Sergen, Fener Cad. 67/1, Kalamış, tel. 3 38 74 74 (midnight)
Yalım, Körfez Cad. 5, Anadoluhisarı, tel. 3 32 00 03 (midnight)

Fish restaurants

Chinese Restaurant, Lamartin Cad. 22/1, Taksim, tel. 1 45 08
19 (11 p.m.)
°Japanese, İstinye Cad. 92, İstinye, tel. 1 65 55 77 (midnight;
Mon.)

Far Eastern specialities

Ancelo, Plaj Gazinosu, Ataköy, tel. 5 71 84 21
Derya, Bostancı, tel. 3 55 16 68 (1 a.m., Tues.)
Mandra, Pangaltı Ergenekon Cad. 73B, tel. 1 48 98 22

Taverns

Bacanak, İstiklâl Cad. 158, Beyoğlu, tel. 1 49 36 56 (midnight)
Piknik, İstiklâl Cad., Taksim, tel. 1 44 67 03 (midnight)
Taksim, Yeni Tarlabaşı Cad., Taksim, tel. 1 45 42 51 (11 p.m.)

Beer-shops

Bars   See Night life

Shipping

Harbour Office   Denizyolları İşletmesi
                                    Rıhtım Caddesi, Karaköy
                                    tel. 1 44 02 07

Shopping and souvenirs

In recent years Istanbul has developed into something of a shopper's paradise. While in the past almost all visitors flocked to the two great bazaars, the Covered Bazaar and the Egyptian Bazaar, they are now increasingly attracted to the elegant shops in the Western-style districts of Beyoğlu, Harbiye, Osmanbey, Nişantaşi and Teşvikiye. The principal shopping streets are İstiklâl Caddesi, Cumhuriyet Caddesi, Halâskargazi Caddesi, Rumeli Caddesi, Şair Nigar Sokaği and Bağdad Caddesi in the district of Erenköy.

Particularly good bargains for Western visitors (thanks to low Turkish wage levels and advantageous exchange rates) are jewellery and precious metals (gold and silver), copper and brass ware, carpets, leather goods (particularly clothes, shoes

A craftsman at work in the Bazaar

and handbags), embroidered cushions, glass (particularly crystal), high-fashion textiles (silk, cotton, virgin wool) and antiques (but buyers should bear in mind the regulations on the export of antiques). An unusual souvenir is a Turkish water-pipe (nargile).

Bazaars:
See A to Z, Kapalı Çarşı
See A to Z, Mısır Çarşısı

Other markets:
The principal markets outside the Bazaar area are in Carşıkapı, Topkapı, Kuledibi and Üsküdar. The wares offered range from the cheapest junk to valuable antiques.

Speciality shops:
Galeri Lebriz, Mim Kemal Öke Cad. 18, Nişantaşı   Antiques
Kerim Eski Eşya ve Sanat Galerisi, Mim Kemal Öke Cad. 11, Nişantaşı
Maksut, Varol, Rumeli Cad./Baytar Ahmen Sok., Nişantaşı
Mustafa ve Yağmur Kayabek, Tünel Pasajı, Beyoğlu
Raffi Portakal, Mim Kemal Öke Cad. 19, Nişantaşı
Troy Antique, Valikonağı Cad. 73, Nişantaşı

Haşet Kitabevi (Hachette), İstiklâl Cad., Beyoğlu   Books
Redhouse Kitabevi, Riza Paşa Yokuşu 50, Uzun Carşı Cad. (Old Town)
Sander Kitabevi, Halâskargazi Cad. 275–277, Osmanbey
Türk-Alman Kitabevi, İstiklâl Cad. 481, Beyoğlu

Bazaar 54, Nuruosmaniye Cad. 54, Cağaloğlu   Carpets

Ayfer, Cumhuriyet Cad. 349, Harbiye   Fashion
Faize Sevim, İlkbelediye Cad., Beyoğlu
Hilmi Kurt, Cumhuriyet Cad. 261, Beyoğlu
İlhan Şerif, Cumhuriyet Cad., Elmadağ
Mefkure Moda Evi, Bağdad Cad., Erenköy
Serdar Butik, Halâskargazi Cad., Kent Pasajı, Osmanbey
Türkan Ergun, Tuğrul Sitesi, Osmanbey

Atilla Mücevherat, Teşvikiye Cad. 153, Nişantaşı   Jewellery
Diamantstein, İstiklâl Cad. 39, Beyoğlu
Diamond, Valikonağı Cad. 3, Nişantaşı
Franguli, İstiklâl Cad. 205, Beyoğlu
Liz Kuyumkusu, Valikonağı Cad. 85, Nişantaşı
Pandantif, Rumeli Cad. 45, Nişantaşı
Prens Mücevherat, Teşvikiye Cad., Nişantaş Pasajı

Deri, Silahhane Cad. 38, Teşvikiye   Leather goods
Divina, Valikonağı Cad. 103, Nişantaşı
Güderimod, Rumeli Cad. 39, Nişantaşı
Güner, Cumhuriyet Cad. 261, Harbiye
Yıldız, İhlamur Yolu Cad., Nişantaşı

Altan Butik, Halâskargazi Cad., Lale Pasajı, Şişli   Shoes
Faruk, Rumeli Cad., Nişantaşı
Goya, İstiklâl Cad. 17, Beyoğlu
Martin, Halâskargazi Cad., Yılmazlar Pasajı, Şişli
Milano, İstiklâl Cad. 51, Beyoğlu
Torino, Rumeli Cad. 55, Nişantaşı

Practical Information

Sightseeing

Information about organised sightseeing tours can be obtained from the official tourist information bureaux (see Information), travel agencies and the larger hotels (see entries).

City tours

A selection of firms which run city sightseeing tours:

İstanbul Vision Aksit
Cumhuriyet Cad. 139/2, Elmadağ, tel. 1 40 54 60

Sultan
Cumhuriyet Cad. 87, Elmadağ, tel. 1 48 60 98

Tur Seyahat
Cumhuriyet Cad. 12C, Elmadağ, tel. 1 47 11 89

Türktur
Cumhuriyet Cad. 193, Harbiye, tel. 1 46 52 56

Guides

The municipal tourist information bureau (see Information) will arrange for the services of a guide, if required. There are also free-lance guides at all the main sites: before engaging one of these, ask for references.

Sport

Stadiums

Mithatpasa Stadyonu
Dolmabahçe

Şişli Stadyonu
Şişli

Fenerbahçe R.C. Stadyonu
Fenerbahçe

Sports hall (indoor)

Spor ve Sergi Sarayı
Harbiye

Golf

Golf Kulübü
Yeni Levent P.K. 73, tel. 1 64 07 42

Riding

Sipahioğlu Binicilik
Gümüşsuyu Cad. 7, Ayazpaşa, tel. 1 44 14 45

Tennis

Tenis-Eskrim-Dağcilik
Askerocağı Cad. 1, Taksim, tel. 1 46 82 50

Tenis Kulübü
Bayıldım Yokuşu 2, Maçka, tel. 1 61 98 99

Shooting

Avcılar-Atcılar İhtisas
Sıraselviler Cad. 58/1, tel. 1 45 19 71

Sailing, water sports

Galatasaray Kulübü
Fenerbahçe, tel. 3 37 54 54

Adalar Kulübü
Burgazada, tel. 3 51 81 07

Suadiye Yat Kulübü
Suadiye, tel. 3 55 23 23

see Yacht harbours

Taxis

Istanbul has hosts of taxis, identified by their striped black and
yellow band. Only a few of them have meters, but fares are
standard for particular distances. Before hiring a taxi make sure
that you agree on the fare.

A dolmuş is a communal taxi running on a particular route. Each   Dolmuş
passenger pays his own fare according to the distance
travelled. There are fixed stopping-places and taxi ranks (e.g.
Taksim, Eminönü, Topkapı), and the fares are fixed by the
municipality. Dolmuşes also run on fixed routes to the airport,
the suburbs of Istanbul and towns in Istanbul province. They
are a reasonably priced alternative to the ordinary taxis.

Telephone, telegrams

Istanbul's telephone service is being modernised; in particular
subscriber trunk dialling (long distance direct dialling) facilities
are being developed.

To the United Kingdom: 99 44   Dialling codes
To the United States or Canada: 99 1

To telephone a telegram dial 04   Telegrams

Theatres

Istanbul has more than two dozen theatres offering varied
performances. The following are worth a visit even if you do not
understand Turkish:

Atatürk Kültür Merkezi   Atatürk Cultural Centre
Taksim Meydanı

Şehir Tiyatrosu   Municipal Theatre
at Radio Evi (Radio House), Harbiye

Devekusu Kabare Tiyatrosu   Cabaret
Straseviler Cad. 91, Taksim

Time

Turkish time is 3 hours ahead of Greenwich Mean Time (8 hours ahead of New York time). Similarly, Turkish summer time is 3 hours ahead of British summer time.

Tipping

A good general rule is to give a tip only for some particular service rendered. Everyone is pleased to have his service recognised. Restaurant bills normally include a service charge of 10–15 per cent, but waiters are given an additional tip of 5–10 per cent.

Travel agencies

A selection of agencies which offer day trips and longer excursions:

ABC Turizm
Cumhuriyet Cad., Gezi Dükkânlar No. 13, Taksim,
tel. 1 43 17 72

Antur
Mecidiyeköy 42C, tel. 1 67 74 78

Bumerang
Rıhtım Cad., Velialemdar Han No. 6/614, Karaköy,
tel. 1 43 55 55

Camel Tours
Dünya Sağlık Sok. 41, Opera İshanı Kat. 5, Taksim,
tel. 1 43 80 20

Istur
Cumhuriyet Cad. 1 Taksim, tel. 1 45 05 75

Tantur
Sheraton Oteli İçi, Taksim, tel. 1 47 85 65

Türk Express
Hilton Oteli, Elmadağ, tel. 1 40 56 40

Ulusoy
Sıraselviler Cad. 16, Taksim, tel. 1 44 28 23

Varan Turizm
İnönü Cad. 17, tel. 1 43 21 87

Travel documents

Nationals of EEC countries, the United States, Canada and most Western countries require only a valid passport to enter

Turkey for a stay of not more than three months. If they are travelling by sea or by road, transit visas will be required for countries passed through (Yugoslavia, Bulgaria).

See Motoring   Car papers

Turkish baths (Hamam)

Given the strict Islamic rules about cleanliness, public bath-houses have been a feature of Turkish life since the Middle Ages. There are usually separate bath-houses for men and women, but if there is only one bath-house in a town it is used by men and women on different days. In the centre of the marble bath hall, which is surrounded by open cabins, is the göbektaşı (belly stone), a marble platform on which the bather, with a towel (peştamal) round his middle, lies to sweat, after which he is rubbed down and massaged by a tellak (for men; a natır for women). This process not only has a cleansing effect but helps the circulation.

Many of the old bath-houses are of great interest in themselves. The following are particularly worth seeing:

Aziziye Hamamı
Rıhtım Cad., Recalzade Sok. 19, Kadıköy, tel. 3 36 17 08
Open daily (men only) 6.30 a.m.–10 p.m.

Cağaloğlu Hamamı
Hilali Ahmer Cad. 34, Cağaloğlu, tel. 5 22 24 24
Open daily 6.30 a.m.–8 p.m. (men), 7.30 a.m.–7.30 p.m. (women)

Galatasaray Hamamı
Turnacibası Sok., tel. 1 49 94 53 (men), 1 49 43 42 (women)
Open daily 6.30 a.m.–10 p.m. (men), 6.30 a.m.–8 p.m. (women)

Water

Istanbul's water is chlorinated and can be drunk without serious risk.

Weights and measures

Turkey uses the metric system.

Yacht harbours (Yat limanları)

The principal yacht harbours are the following:

Bebek, Büyükdere and Tarabya Bays   Bosphorus

Kalamış Bay (south of Haydarpaşa)   Sea of Marmara

Burgaz Ada, Büyük Ada   Princes' Islands

Youth hostels (Hosteller)

IYHF Youth Hostel
Cerrahpaşa Cad. 63, Aksaray, tel. 1 43 00 08

Topkapı Atatürk Öğrenci Sitesi
Londra Asfaltı, Topkapı, tel. 5 25 50 32

Yücel Tourist Hotel
Sultanahmet, tel. 5 22 45 01

Useful Telephone Numbers

Emergencies
  Police, ambulance

    1 66 66 66 (all parts of city)
    5 21 15 95 (Stamboul)
    1 44 49 98 (Beyoğlu/Taksim)
    3 33 04 01 (Üsküdar)

  Fire

    55 24 11 24 (Stamboul)
    1 40 77 77 (Beyoğlu/Taksim)
    3 33 20 30 (Üsküdar)

  Breakdown assistance (TTOK)

    1 46 70 90, 5 21 65 88
    (during day only)

  Military police   05
  Tourist police   5 28 53 69

Information
  Ministry of Tourism and Information   1 45 68 75
  Municipal Information Bureau   5 26 21 00
  Turizm Danisma, Sultanahmet   5 27 21 88
  Turkish Touring and Automobile Club (TTOK)   1 46 70 90
  Telephone news   1 66 99 20
  Public transport (IETT)   1 46 81 30
  Train information, Europe   5 27 00 50
  Train information, Asia   3 36 04 75
  Harbour Office   44 02 07
  Duty doctors and chemists   01

Lost property offices
  Public transport (IETT)   1 46 81 31
  Sirkeci Station   5 27 00 51
  Haydarpaşa Station   3 36 20 63
  Town Hall   5 26 21 00

Telephone
  Dialling code to the United Kingdom   99 44
  Dialling code to the United States or Canada   99 1
  Long-distance calls (rapid connection)   09
  To telephone a telegram   04

Baedeker's Travel Guides

"The maps and illustrations are lavish. The arrangement of information (alphabetically by city) makes it easy to use the book."
—*San Francisco Examiner-Chronicle*

What's there to do and see in foreign countries? Travelers who rely on Baedeker, one of the oldest names in travel literature, will miss nothing. Baedeker's bright red, internationally recognized covers open up to reveal fascinating A-Z directories of cities, towns, and regions, complete with their sights, museums, monuments, cathedrals, castles, gardens and ancestral homes—an approach that gives the traveler a quick and easy way to plan a vacation itinerary.

And Baedekers are filled with over 200 full colour photos and detailed maps, including a full-size, fold-out roadmap for easy vacation driving. Baedeker—the premier name in travel for over 150 years.

Please send me the books checked below:

☐ **Austria**..............................$15.95 0–13–056127–4	☐ **Mediterranean Islands**.......$14.95 0–13–056862–7
☐ **Caribbean**.........................$15.95 0–13–056143–6	☐ **Mexico**...............................$15.95 0–13–056069–3
☐ **Denmark**............................$14.95 0–13–058124–0	☐ **Netherlands, Belgium and** **Luxembourg**.....................$14.95 0–13–056028–6
☐ **Egypt**.................................$15.95 0–13–056358–7	☐ **Portugal**.............................$15.95 0–13–056135–5
☐ **France**................................$15.95 0–13–055814–1	☐ **Provence/Côte d'Azur**..........$9.95 0–13–056938–0
☐ **Germany**............................$15.95 0–13–055830–3	☐ **Rail Guide to Europe**..........$15.95 0–13–055971–7
☐ **Great Britain**......................$15.95 0–13–055855–9	☐ **Rhine**..................................$9.95 0–13–056466–4
☐ **Greece**...............................$14.95 0–13–056002–2	☐ **Scandinavia**.......................$15.95 0–13–056085–5
☐ **Greek Islands**.....................$10.95 0–13–058132–1	☐ **Spain**.................................$15.95 0–13–055913–X
☐ **Ireland**...............................$15.95 0–13–058140–2	☐ **Switzerland**........................$15.95 0–13–056044–8
☐ **Israel**.................................$15.95 0–13–056176–2	☐ **Turkish Coast**....................$10.95 0–13–058173–9
☐ **Italy**...................................$15.95 0–13–055897–4	☐ **Tuscany**..............................$9.95 0–13–056482–6
☐ **Japan**.................................$15.95 0–13–056382–X	☐ **Yugoslavia**.........................$15.95 0–13–056184–3
☐ **Loire**...................................$9.95 0–13–056375–7	

Please turn the page for an order form and a list of additional Baedeker Guides.

A series of city guides filled with color photographs and detailed maps and floor plans from one of the oldest names in travel publishing:

Please send me the books checked below:

☐ **Amsterdam**..............................$10.95
0–13–057969–6

☐ **Athens**....................................$10.95
0–13–057977–7

☐ **Bangkok**..................................$10.95
0–13–057985–8

☐ **Berlin**......................................$10.95
0–13–367996–9

☐ **Brussels**..................................$10.95
0–13–368788–0

☐ **Budapest**.................................$10.95
0–13–058199–2

☐ **Cologne**...................................$10.95
0–13–058181–X

☐ **Copenhagen**.............................$10.95
0–13–057993–9

☐ **Florence**...................................$10.95
0–13–369505–0

☐ **Frankfurt**.................................$10.95
0–13–369570–0

☐ **Hamburg**..................................$10.95
0–13–369687–1

☐ **Hong Kong**...............................$10.95
0–13–058009–0

☐ **Istanbul**...................................$10.95
0–13–058207–7

☐ **Jerusalem**................................$10.95
0–13–058017–1

☐ **London**.....................................$10.95
0–13–058025–2

☐ **Madrid**.....................................$10.95
0–13–058033–3

☐ **Moscow**....................................$10.95
0–13–058041–4

☐ **Munich**.....................................$10.95
0–13–370370–3

☐ **New York**.................................$10.95
0–13–058058–9

☐ **Paris**.......................................$10.95
0–13–058066–X

☐ **Prague**.....................................$10.95
0–13–058215–8

☐ **Rome**.......................................$10.95
0–13–058074–0

☐ **San Francisco**..........................$10.95
0–13–058082–1

☐ **Singapore**................................$10.95
0–13–058090–2

☐ **Stuttgart**.................................$10.95
0–13–058223–9

☐ **Tokyo**......................................$10.95
0–13–058108–9

☐ **Venice**.....................................$10.95
0–13–058116–X

☐ **Vienna**.....................................$10.95
0–13–371303–2

PRENTICE HALL PRESS
Order Department—Travel Books
200 Old Tappan Road
Old Tappan, New Jersey 07675
In U.S. include $1 postage and handling for 1st book, 25¢ each additional book.
Outside U.S. $2 and 50¢ respectively.

Enclosed is my check or money order for $_____

NAME_____

ADDRESS_____

CITY_____STATE_____ZIP_____